PERFECT PHRASES™

for

PERFORMANCE
REVIEWS

PERFECT PHRASES™

for

PERFORMANCE REVIEWS

second edition

**Hundreds of Ready-to-Use Phrases for
Describing Employee Performance**

Douglas Max and Robert Bacal

New York Chicago San Francisco Lisbon London Madrid Mexico City
Milan New Delhi San Juan Seoul Singapore Sydney Toronto

Copyright © 2011 by The McGraw-Hill Companies, Inc. Printed in the United States of America. Except as permitted under the United States Copyright Act of 1976, no part of this publication may be reproduced or distributed in any form or by any means, or stored in a database or retrieval system, without the prior written permission of the publisher.

1 2 3 4 5 6 7 8 9 10   QFR/QFR   1 9 8 7 6 5 4 3 2 1 0

ISBN 978-0-07-174507-9
MHID   0-07-174507-6

Library of Congress Cataloging-in-Publication Data

Max, Douglas.
    Perfect phrases for performance reviews / by Douglas Max — 2nd ed.
      p. cm.
    Rev. ed. of Perfect phrases for performance reviews : hundreds of ready-to-use phrases that describe your employees' performance (from unacceptable to outstanding) / Douglas Max, Robert Bacal. 2003.
    ISBN 978-0-07-174507-9 (alk. paper)
    1. Employees—Rating of. 2. Employees—Rating of—Terminology. I. Title.
    HF5549.5.R3M258 2011
    658.3'125—dc22

                        2010029964

This is a *CWL Publishing Enterprises Book* produced for McGraw-Hill by CWL Publishing Enterprises, Inc., Madison, Wisconsin, www.cwlpub.com.

McGraw-Hill books are available at special quantity discounts to use as premiums and sales promotions, or for use in corporate training programs. To contact a representative, please e-mail us at bulksales@mcgraw-hill.com.

This book is printed on acid-free paper.

Contents

Contents

Part Three. Perfect Phrases for Performance Reviews

Topics Listed Alphabetically

Contents

Contents

Topics by Job Category

General Job Skills/Traits

Technical Skills

Contents

Appendix A. Ten Mistakes Managers Make When Conducting Performance Appraisals   197

Appendix B. Seven Mistakes Employees Make During Performance Appraisals   201

The Most Important Preface You Will Ever Read

When McGraw-Hill approached us to do a second edition of this book, we had mixed feelings. The first edition was a commercial success, even having landed on the *BusinessWeek* bestseller list. On the other hand, we were truly perplexed. How could we make this book more useful to managers, supervisors, and HR personnel? After all, there is only so much you can do with short phrases describing employee performance.

To do "more of the same" seemed pointless and to a writer, it's not only frustrating, but it's pretty dull stuff.

We also had some concerns that books of phrases and their *misuse* was inconsistent with our approach to performance management as a cooperative process that is conducted during the entire year and is characterized by effective goal-setting, ongoing communication, and removing barriers to performance so that everybody gains.

The Task: How to Make It Better *and* Unique

After looking at other books containing performance review phrases, it struck me that they all suffer from the same malady—

a significant illness that has been pointed out by others. Performance reviews look at the past and not the present and the future, so as someone once said, "Performance reviews are like driving while looking only in the rearview mirror." Describing past behavior is simply not good enough, if that's as far as things go. And, yes, if you are wondering, the first edition of this book shared that fault.

What if we could modify the book to get across the idea that performance reviews are for the purpose of improving perform- ance and removing barriers to performance, and *not* hammering on employee faults in the often-forgotten past.

Once we shifted *our* perspective, the pieces fell into place. Why not include phrases to use during reviews that focus on the future *and* encourage employee self-evaluation? The latter came out in conversations with managers about the kind of employ- ees they valued. Managers want employees who can self-modify their behavior and evaluate how they are doing. When employ- ees learn to do this, the gains in productivity and the managerial time saved are simply huge.

What Did We Change?

Virtually every page in this book has been edited, improved, and modified. We've learned over the years and have been able to write different kinds of performance descriptors ranging from the gen- eral to the more specific and quantitative, and that's all reflected in this edition.

We also added and "modernized" things to reflect changes in the workplace that have taken place in the last 10 years.

The major and most profound changes have to do with two new sections for each set of performance phrases.

First we added questions and statements to use to *promote employee self-evaluation*. This puts the evaluation ball at least partly in the court of each employee, and that is as it should be. You don't want to be doing something to the employee. You want to work *with* the employee.

Second, we added a section for each set of statements, called "Looking Forward," which includes phrases and questions about how to improve future performance, again pushing the employee to take responsibility for his or her performance improvement.

What you hold in your hand can still be used to describe past behavior, and yes, it is an improved tool for that. The real leap, though, lies in looking forward, which is what is required to make performance reviews a powerful management tool.

These changes make this book special and unique.

So Why Is This the Most Important Preface You Will Ever Read?

If you're a manager who cannot see the point of doing performance reviews because they never seem to improve performance, it's time to take a look at alternatives. By using the additions to this book you can start "driving" your organization by looking in front of you, not behind you.

If you are a manager looking to shortcut the review process by picking semi-relevant phrases from some book written by two fellows you have never met, it's time to reevaluate. If that's all you want, it's here, but we promise you, you are wasting valuable time and shortchanging yourself and your employees.

Pay attention to this. Most of us have never seen an effective performance management/review system so it is not surprising that we have limited expectations or even wear our appraisal cynicism on our sleeves. Now is the time to change.

You have the opportunity to be a better manager, improve productivity and morale, involve and engage staff, and remove the discomforts of performance reviews.

Look Forward, Not Backward

Don't expect canned phrases to solve your problems or improve performance.

Work with your employees to help them learn what you want, and how to self-evaluate their own progress.

Be involved *with* your staff, and stop doing things to them.

If you make these simple changes, you'll be amazed at how much easier the function of management becomes.

Let's face it. We are coming through a period of difficult economic times, and we need our companies, organizations, and employees firing on all cylinders. Poor, halfhearted attempts at performance reviews are a luxury we cannot afford.

We think this book will help.

Of course only our readers can evaluate how well we have accomplished our goals. To this end, feel free to drop us a line via e-mail at ceo@work911.com to let us know how we've done.

Who knows? Maybe in a few years there will be a third edition of this book, and we'd like to incorporate your suggestions and ideas in it.

Good luck.

Acknowledgments

This book started with John Woods of CWL Publishing Enterprises asking us to take it on. We did, and it has been a hit in the marketplace, for which we want to express our thanks to John and all of those who found it useful. John is still working with us in the creation of this second edition, along with Brian Foster at McGraw-Hill. Marg Sumner and Kelly Tomkies helped with the final proofreading. We thank them all for their help in creating the book you now hold.

—Douglas Max and Robert Bacal

Part One

Background for Conducting Performance Reviews

How to Plan, Conduct, and Write a Performance Review

Undertaking formal performance appraisals is not an activity most managers relish, but it's an important part of the job of a manager. You have an opportunity, by reviewing performance effectively, to directly and positively affect the future productivity of your employees. Conducting an effective appraisal means more than just filling out the form your company uses, however. What goes on before you fill out the form is critical to getting the results you're looking for.

If all you want to do is get forms filled out, skip ahead to Part Two. If you want to accomplish something worthwhile that will make your life easier, continue reading

As part of the appraisal process in many organizations, the manager and employee have a meeting where the manager explains the appraisal process and the criteria for judging performance. If the process involves goals, the manager and employee discuss and agree on what they both would like to see achieved over a certain time period (usually a year) and, perhaps, the kind of resources the employee will need to succeed. If you are responsible for defining employee goals, then use the initial meeting to explain these goals (and how you will work together to achieve those goals, if appropriate).

Throughout the year, document significant behaviors that are worthy of discussion during a performance review. Keep notes as you observe the performance of your employees. It's simple and easy to do—far easier than waiting until the end of the year and then trying to recollect what happened.

Setting Performance Goals

What is a goal? It's an agreed-upon statement of what an employee will achieve in a specified period. A goals statement should also outline the resources necessary to achieve the goals and how you and your employee will measure success.

Each goal should be measurable, attainable, moderately difficult, and accepted by the employee. Here are some examples:

- Number of rejected items from manufacturing line will not exceed 0.3 percent per week.
- Sales per quarter will increase by 5 percent.
- Expense account will not exceed budget.
- Sign up five new customers per month.

In other words, goals should be measurable and aimed at improving the performance of the employee. Well, so the theory goes. Actually the tricky part is "measurable." It turns out that the things that are easy to measure are usually trivial, and the things that are hard to measure are what separate a good employee from a lesser one. That doesn't mean we give up on measurable goals. It does mean that perfection is not possible.

Why do we write goals? Written goals allow you to both measure and recognize achievement. They also let you identify and correct performance problems, and they enable you to identify and focus on your top priorities. Aim to limit the number of long-term goals to no more than five. You can write additional short-term goals for projects that can be completed in a few weeks or months.

How do you write goals? To write goals, you first need to collect information from your own records and those of your employees. The next section explains the kind of information you might use.

What kind of information will you need? You and your employees can best answer this question because it depends on the specific situation and each job. Some guidelines:

Most goals that relate to productivity are generally expressed in terms that include:

- Volume of work
- Accuracy of work
- Time to produce X
- Cost per unit of X

Volume measures the amount of work performed, for example, the number of:

- Orders entered
- Cartons packed
- Requisitions written
- Documents filed

Accuracy measures the degree to which the work is performed free of error, or the quality of the work, for example, the percentage of:

- Orders entered accurately vs. inaccurately
- Cartons packed correctly vs. incorrectly
- Requisitions written correctly vs. incorrectly
- Documents filed accurately vs. inaccurately

Time measures the duration of work performed, per hour, per day, per week, per month, or per year. Examples include:

- Claims processed per hour/day/week
- Requisitions received and written on the first day/second day/third day
- Documents received and filed on the first day/second day/third day

Cost measures the dollars spent for work performed. For example:

$$\frac{\text{Average number of orders per day by the department}}{\text{Average daily wage for department}} = y$$

$$\frac{\text{Average number of claims processed per day by employee}}{\text{Average hourly wage for department}} = y$$

$$\text{Number of requisition errors resulting in rewrites} \times \text{Cost per rewrite} = y$$

What if goal achievement is difficult to measure? There may be times when an employee has goals that you cannot easily measure. This does not mean that you should not have such goals. Just be certain to have some criteria for evaluating the level of achievement. Here are some examples:

- **Monthly reports.** "Performance is acceptable when I turn in completed monthly reports no more than two times late in any four-month period, without more than one incident of it being more than one week late in any six-month period, and when it is accepted by my boss in all cases with no more than two revisions that are completed in no more than one week."

- **Forecasting.** "I will not fail to bring to my boss's attention adverse trends in my performance before the failure point is reached. This will happen no more than two times in any 12-month period."
- **Employee development.** "Performance is acceptable when training, motivation, and appraisal are discussed during at least two meetings annually between me and each of my direct reports."

Documenting Critical Incidents and Significant Behaviors

An important part of the appraisal process involves recording incidents and behaviors that are out of the ordinary. These are referred to as "critical incidents" and "significant behaviors." A critical incident is behavior that is usually extreme (either good or bad) and that should be recorded for legal reasons, for disciplinary measures, or for purposes of recognizing exemplary actions "above and beyond the call of duty." A significant behavior is one that can make a real difference in an employee's performance.

There are many reasons you should keep a record of employees' significant behaviors:

- It increases the accuracy of the performance appraisal, because it's based on documentation rather than memory.
- It provides evidence to support ratings.
- It helps guarantee that you'll consider the performance during the entire appraisal period.

■ It reduces bias that occurs when you rate only the most recent behavior.

To be as accurate as possible, write down significant behaviors as soon as possible after you have observed the behavior. Record only the specific behavioral facts of the case. Do not include opinions. Do not rely on hearsay! To ensure that the documentation is a representative record of an individual's performance, document performance during the entire appraisal period.

In documenting behaviors, be consistent in how you do it. Use the same format and the same level of detail with each individual. Document both productive and unproductive behaviors. Documenting significant behaviors helps to make the performance evaluation interview more productive. You'll be more confident going into the interview if you have a record of behaviors to back up your ratings because you'll be more confident you're rating your employee accurately.

Documenting significant behavior helps improve communication in the interview. There is less likelihood of disagreement about whether an event occurred when you have documented behaviors and incidents. It helps keep the tone of the entire appraisal constructive rather than judgmental. Instead of dealing with impressions, you're dealing with specific examples of performance. The discussion can focus on how the performance can be improved in the future. Employees are better able to see their deficiencies. They know what they must do to improve.

The feedback to employees, both positive and critical, about significant behaviors can enhance employee motivation to improve. When an employee sees that specific behaviors are noted and appreciated, he or she will feel good and work harder to generate such feedback. In the case of behaviors that undermine performance, the employee may not be aware of the problems. Here are some examples of significant behaviors you might note:

- Customer called after hours with urgent need for a replacement part to deal with an emergency situation. Employee personally delivered part, substantially reinforcing the loyalty of an important customer.
- Made specific suggestion on manufacturing process that resulted in $50,000 in savings over a six-month period.
- Angrily reacted to an incident on the shop floor that intimidated other employees and made it more difficult to investigate what happened.

Accurate documentation of specific behavior and incidents allows an employee to understand which on-the-job behaviors are productive and which are not. Such information gives employees what they need to improve.

Writing the Appraisal

If you've collected significant behaviors during this appraisal period, then the first step in writing an appraisal that will result in improved or continued good performance is to review these notes. Review also any results or other metrics you have to judge how well the employee has met his or her goals.

Even if your appraisal form only calls for you to "check a box," you generally can add comments to justify or explain the rating. In fact, if the appraisal process is to have any value to the employee, you must provide more information than a numeric rating. If you aren't required to make comments, you may want to consider including them on the appraisal form anyway.

Combined with the significant behavior statements and actual work results, you're most of the way to completing a form and documenting an effective appraisal.

Common Performance Review Errors

Another thing you'll want to do is to review the common errors made during the appraisal process. It's a bit more complicated than you think—the business of providing fair and objective feedback to employees—because . . . well, you're human. You can easily avoid or reduce errors by understanding what errors are common and following the suggestions below for dealing with them.

Contrast Error. The tendency to evaluate a person relative to other individuals, rather than basing the evaluation on the requirements of the job. An example would be rating someone low, even though he or she was above average, because everyone else in the department is superior. A review should be based on comparing performance with established criteria.

First-Impression Error. The tendency to make an initial favorable or unfavorable judgment, which then serves as the basis for appraising future performance. All subsequent information is ignored or perceptually distorted. By considering behavior throughout the rating period, you'll reduce this error.

Recency Effect. The tendency to give extra weight to what you have seen recently and diminish the importance of observations you may have made earlier in the review period. In some cases it may be appropriate to weigh recent behavior more than old behavior, particularly if it shows improvement. Otherwise, be sure to consider the entire period of appraisal.

Halo Effect. Generalizing from one aspect of performance to all aspects of performance. People have strengths and weaknesses. It is important to evaluate all aspects of performance throughout the period of the review.

Devil Effect. The opposite of the halo effect, generalizing from one or two negative aspects of performance and becoming blind to the positive aspects of the performance.

Similar-to-Me Effect. The tendency to judge more favorably those people whose background is similar to yours. The more similar the attitudes and background, the greater the tendency to judge that individual favorably. Appraise performance and behaviors, not personality or background.

Central Tendency. Occurs when an employee is consistently rated at or near the midpoint of the scale, regardless of the actual level of performance. This is a problem for several reasons. Such evaluations don't differentiate between good and bad performers. They're particularly damaging to the motivation of high achievers, and they don't provide a realistic basis for discussing actual performance and improvements during the appraisal discussion.

Negative or Positive Leniency. Occurs when an employee is rated too hard (negative leniency) or too easy (positive leniency). Again, it creates a problem because the appraisal doesn't reflect true performance. With negative leniency, good performers may get tired of trying to perform well; no matter what they do, they'll be rated lower. With positive leniency, employees may have unrealistic expectations about raises, promotions, or other career gains.

To reduce rating errors:

- Ensure the criteria being used are job-related.
- Rate employees in relation to the job responsibilities.
- Put other people's input into proper perspective and don't weigh it too heavily. If you feel that this additional input warrants changes in the appraisal, discuss it with your boss.
- Consider all performance dimensions and realize that they are not always related. A person can do very well on one dimension and perform poorly on another.
- Don't rate people in any particular order. Don't rate all the best or worst performers first.
- Don't compare the ratings of employees until after all employee evaluations are complete.

Legal Issues

When an employment situation becomes a legal situation, there's no substitute for proof—you must have records or other evidence proving that an employee did or did not do something, whether it's stealing, lying, or being late too many times.

What may be more important is that you document the communication you have with employees, particularly when it involves discussion of performance problems. Generally, if you have not notified or discussed problems with the employee and documented those discussions, you have less backup if the employee accuses you of discrimination or similar charges. That means ensuring that the employee signs any documents you keep about your communication with the employee.

Be alert for performance that's out of the ordinary, either good or bad, and make a note of it. That way, when it comes time to do the appraisal review, you'll be prepared, and you'll be similarly prepared for court, should it ever come to that. The best way to deal with legal issues is to prevent them by conducting a competent, fair appraisal, demonstrating that you've invested a lot of time analyzing this employee's performance. Then conduct the review as we suggest, and you'll substantially minimize the chances that your conduct would lead to a lawsuit or other legal action. Here are some specifics to remember:

- Keep copies of HR records even if the HR department also has these records.
- Maintain accurate performance data.
- Meet regularly with employees to provide the feedback and information they need to perform well, also reducing any surprises and the motivation to sue.
- Document, document, document.

Conducting the Review

How to talk about your employees' performance. The first thing you can do to conduct an effective performance appraisal is to make sure there are no surprises in store for the employee. This means you should have communicated with your employees on a regular basis about how they are doing with their particular assignments and how they are collaborating with others.

The formal appraisal session should be mainly a way to summarize and continue the informal interaction that has previously taken place between you and your employees. It should also be a time to look at how you and the employee can continue to work well together in the future. Your job in this session is not to tell the employee all the things you think he or she did wrong over the past year. One reason performance appraisal sessions are often dreaded is that managers and employees feel the managers have to find something to criticize about the person being appraised. What can happen in that situation is that the manager might mention a negative comment the employee made or the fact that the employee was late to work two times over the past six months or similar trivial points. This causes employees to feel resentful and become defensive, and it adds nothing to their motivation to improve performance.

Approach the person you're appraising as a partner rather than a judge. This minimizes hostility. Also, by focusing on your employee's development rather than on fault finding, you'll set a positive tone and the discussion becomes more productive and easier for both of you.

You may be conducting a performance review because it's required, but it's also a great opportunity to help your employees achieve job goals. Talk with your employees one-on-one about your expectations for them. Talk about goals, resources to help them achieve these goals, and what you're planning on doing to help. With some, you'll set goals to meet certain performance results; with others, you might set target levels for different "ratings"; for others, the goals might be related to on-the-job behavior; for others still, the goals might target both behaviors and results.

Set goals, work toward them with your employees, and discuss what worked or did not work at the next review. That's easier said than done! Nevertheless, employees want to know where they stand. They want to receive feedback on their performance. Both ongoing discussions and periodic performance appraisals enable you to provide employees with this information.

Tell them the purpose. Since performance helps determine salary, job assignments, transfers, promotions, demotions, and termination, it is important to tell the employee that you're rating his or her performance based on responsibilities and goals.

The appraisal discussion is also a time to discuss the employee's job expectations and the organization's expectations of the employee. You should also encourage the employee to talk about any other job-related issues or concerns.

Minimize reluctance. Many employees are not enthusiastic about performance appraisals because previous ones seemed "a waste of time" or unpleasant. Your skill determines whether employees regard the discussion with enthusiasm or dread. You can change their attitudes by listening to their concerns, explaining how you plan to handle the meeting, and that the main purpose of the meeting is to help you both improve.

Gain the employee's commitment. You want the employee to actively participate in the entire appraisal process. This can happen if the employee understands that it will be a two-way discussion of performance. The employee should also understand that the purpose of the appraisal is to recognize success and plan improvement where necessary.

To ensure your appraisal meeting is successful, review the recommendations below and follow the steps outlined later to help guide you through the meeting.

- Discuss actual performance data/significant behaviors.
- Compare data with responsibilities/goals.
- Rate performance (if appropriate in your appraisal system).
- Maintain a positive focus.
- Focus on solving problems, not finding fault.
- Solicit and use input from employees.
- Evaluate objectively.

- Provide recognition.
- Discuss specific actions for you and the employee to take.
- Express confidence.

Discuss actual performance data/significant behaviors. If the performance appraisal discussion is to be effective, you should have performance data and significant behaviors for each area of measurement. The employee should have access to this same data before the appraisal session. Both you and the employee must feel that the data is objective and accurate. If the employee reviews the data prior to the appraisal, you can handle questions about its objectivity and accuracy before the appraisal discussion.

Compare data with responsibilities/goals. This way both you and the employee know whether he or she has met, exceeded, or missed the goals for the job. Before the session in some organizations, it's the employee's responsibility to also prepare data on goal achievement.

Rate performance. Rate the employee's performance in each area of measurement, based on actual data. The ratings should take into account any factors outside the employee's control that contributed to achieving or failing to achieve his or her goals. It's a good idea to discuss your ratings with your immediate supervisor so that both of you are confident that your ratings are justifiable.

Maintain a positive focus. If the employee's overall performance rating is satisfactory, the emphasis of feedback should be that he or she is doing well. Allow sufficient time to discuss and recognize those areas where performance met or exceeded goals. Exploring the factors that led to success will help you and the employee build on strengths to increase productivity.

Focus on solving problems, not finding fault. In those areas where the employee is not meeting expectations with regard to responsibilities or goals, the emphasis should be on identifying the causes, focusing on solutions, and outlining specific actions that will enable the employee to meet those expectations. The discussion should be future-oriented, focusing on plans for improvement. Expression of concern with past poor performance should be balanced with recognition of achievements, if overall performance is satisfactory.

Solicit and use input from employees. You should actively involve the employee in the performance appraisal discussion. In addition to sharing performance data and participating in the problem-solving discussion, the employee may also have additional items or concerns to discuss. Be prepared to discuss these items openly and work toward solutions. The employee may want to discuss salary, career opportunities, or barriers to satisfactory performance, such as insufficient resources, lack of management support, etc. If you cannot adequately address such issues during the appraisal discussion, you should set a follow-up date to discuss these items at length.

Evaluate objectively. This means you're focusing on performance and the factors that led to success or the obstacles that got in the way of success. You are not evaluating the person but his or her performance in a fair and dispassionate way. If the employee knows this is what you are doing and that both of you are there to help each other succeed, the session will be much more productive.

Provide recognition. Praise the employee for those things done well. When you praise, you're helping the person know what he or she is doing well so that he or she will continue to do those things. It also creates a positive tone for the session.

Discuss specific actions for you and the employee to take. At the conclusion of the session, list specific actions the employee will take to finish old business, take on new goals, and improve his or her skills. Also list the actions you will take to support the employee in these activities.

Express confidence. Let the employee know you feel good about his or her abilities, you're there to help the employee succeed, and you're confident that by working together this will happen, and you are glad to be working with him or her.

Making the Session Go Smoothly

As you undertake the appraisal, here are some ways you can make the actual session go smoothly:

- Put the employee at ease at the start of the session. Do this by acknowledging that these sessions can be a little nerve-wracking, but that the purpose is to help everyone in the work group improve and to gather information on how to help the improvement efforts.
- Ask the employee what he or she thinks of his or her total performance—not just strong or weak areas. In this way, you get an overall sense of how the employee thinks he or she is doing.
- Question the employee about what he or she thinks his or her personal strengths are. This chance to describe what he or she does best helps the employee feel positive about the appraisal.

- Tell the employee what you believe his or her strengths are. This demonstrates that you are paying attention to performance.
- Describe those areas where you think the employee might improve; use documentation to demonstrate why you are making these observations. Then ask the employee what he or she thinks of this and listen silently to the response. His or her reasons for poor performance or problems on the job might include lack of training, personality conflicts with other employees, misunderstandings about expectations or responsibilities, lack of knowledge about how to use new equipment, and physical obstacles, such as poor lighting or poorly maintained equipment.
- Assuming you can identify the cause of poor performance, ask the employee what the two of you can do together to take care of it.
- Set new goals for performance for the next appraisal period.
- Keep a record of the meeting, including a timetable for performance improvement and what each of you will do to ensure that happens.
- Be open and honest, yet considerate of the employee's feelings. The goal is to facilitate improvement for the individual, the team, and the organization.

After the appraisal session, it's vital to follow up on what you and the employee have agreed on during the session. It indicates that you and the organization are serious about improvement.

- Mark your calendar to meet with individual employees to review their progress.

- Set up training as needed to address skill deficiencies.
- If a personal problem is involved, arrange for the employee to get counseling, if it's available.
- If an employee continues to perform poorly, make him or her aware of the consequences (discipline, demotion, or termination).
- Provide positive feedback when you see improvements in performance.

How to Talk About Salary

Performance reviews are often held as separate meetings from discussions about salary. If it's this way in your company, then you should explain that to the employee, as well as the reasons for doing it this way.

Presumably it's because the focus of the discussion is performance and not money, which will be considered at another time. You may, though, be able to tell employees more, such as that their performance was superior and that it will bring them nearer the higher bonuses or that their overall performance was below par, and so that's approximately what they might expect with their bonuses.

If an employee is adamant about discussing salary and it's against the policy in your company, then you should schedule a meeting to discuss that topic.

Perfect Phrases for Performance Reviews

When documenting performance or justifying the rating you've given an employee, focus on behaviors and results. Work on finding a phrase that best describes how you judge the person's performance in a particular area. Helping you do that is the purpose of this book, but you should, of course, modify these phrases to fit your particular situation. Since there are many related categories in the phrases in Part Three, be sure to check all appropriate categories to find phrases that will work best for you in a particular situation.

For example, take a phrase like "exceedingly competent." Delete "exceedingly" and you're left with "competent." Substitute "not very," "sometimes," etc., and you've got an entirely different meaning—something that may more accurately reflect the shade of meaning you're looking for.

There are two types of phrases or items in each category. One type describes that characteristic in general terms; the other type includes some more behavioral or results-oriented phrases you might use in the appraisal. For these behavioral items, you should, of course, include your own terms, numbers, etc., and place them under the appropriate rating on the form you're using.

You might also use these concrete items to establish goals or as the basis for creating a rating scale. For example, you'll give an employee an "outstanding" or a "5" rating if she makes 1 percent or fewer errors, an "exceeds expectations" or "4" for 2 percent–5 percent errors, and so on.

Part Two

Examples of Forms for Performance Reviews

Performance Review Forms

The purpose of this book is to provide you with hundreds of phrases to facilitate the performance appraisal process. In keeping with that goal, this part of the book includes a few examples of appraisal forms used in three organizations. All of these differ, yet they all require the person doing the appraising to include descriptive phrases such as those found in Part Three.

We have edited and reformatted these forms to fit this book. The parts of the forms that would use phrases like those included in this book are filled in. The other parts are included so you can see the entire form, including instructions on one of them that define levels of performance and the parts that require the manager and employee to put down their thoughts and goals for the next review period. Use these examples for models as you use this book to undertake your appraisals.

Example 1

Performance Expectations/Review

Key Results Expected:

10 percent reduction in waste
Five suggestions for improvement from all employees
and so on

Key Job Competencies:

Competency Group	Competency	Examples/Comments
Communication	Facilitate Communication	Effectively builds interactivity with others
	Oral Communication	Articulate and well-organized
	Written Communication	Writes quickly, clearly, and correctly
Continuous Improvement	Initiative and innovation	Is above the norm in showing initiative
	Flexibility	Will reset priorities as required
	Technical Expertise	Has mastered SPC techniques
Leadership	Leadership	Led group to exceed sales targets in 14 of 15 regions
	Empowering Others	Turns on the motivation for excellece among employees
	Use of Influence	Demeanor sets an example for others
	Coaching	Delivers feedback directly and constructively
Teamwork	Professional Conduct	Manages the team process with great skill
	Responsiveness	Keeps others informed of status of projects affecting them

We have discussed and agreed upon the above performance competencies.

_____   _____
Employee Signature   **Manager Signature**

Example 2

Performance Planning and Review Document	
Employee Name: _____	Position Title: _____
Hire Date: _____	Review Date: _____
Department: _____	Supervisor's Name: _____

Items for Discussion	Supervisor's Comments (Required)
Professionalism	
Attitude	Direct, straightforward, and honest. Always focuses on getting things done.
Acceptance of Responsibility	Willingly accepts responsibility for new projects.
Dependability	Always delivers on promises.
Work	
Job Knowledge	Maintains knowledge through training and seminars.
Work Quality	Quality of outputs meets standards.
Customer Service	Solves customer problems with speed and accuracy.
Communication	Articulate and well-organized speaker.
Teamwork	Mostly an optimistic team player.
Flexibility	Able to shift focus rapidly.
Safe/Unsafe Work Practices	Has violated a safety rule only once.
Optional Factors	
Employee Input Form	
Attached and Discussed	

(continued)

Example 2 *(continued)*

Performance Planning and Review Document
Additional Comments by Supervisor:
Comments by Employee:
Other performance issues discussed during this review period: _____ **Yes, please indicate if other documentation exists** _____ **No**
Supervisors and employees are required to sign the form. Signatures indicate that the supervisor and employee have discussed performance and the comments written on this document. Signatures do not necessarily indicate agreement.

Supervisor Signature: **Date:**

Employee Signature: **Date:**

Next-Level Supervisor Signature: **Date:**

Example 3

Performance Appraisal

Employee's Name: Title:

Review Period __/__/__ to __/__/__   Employee SSN:

Work Location: Supervisor's Name:

Type of Review ____ 90 day   ____Performance

INSTRUCTIONS

1. **Rating:** Rate the employee in each job area, unless it is not applicable, by placing the rating in the box that best indicates where the employee stands in relation to the accountability. Every factor must be either rated or marked "NA/NO" (Not applicable/ Not observed). Indicate the overall rating at the end of the job areas.

2. **Remarks:** Use the "Remarks" space after each job area to explain in more detail or to give examples of that area. All areas except level 3 require comments.

3. **Summary:** Complete the Major Accomplishments, Job-Related Strengths, Areas for Improvement/Development, Action Plan sections. Have the employee complete the Employee Comments section. Use additional sheets if needed.

4. **Human Resources Review:** Human Resources must review and sign the evaluation before the actual review is conducted.

5. **Signatures:** Sign the review and have the employee sign before submitting the original form to Human Resources for filing in the employee's personnel file.

Ratings and Meanings:

5 Performance consistently exceeds job requirements. Demonstrates unusually high level of performance relative to all assignments and objectives. Distinguished performance overall.

4 Performance meets and often exceeds job requirements. Demonstrates successful performance on all major assignments and objectives and consistently exceeds position requirements in some areas.

3 Performance consistently meets job requirements. Demonstrates successful performance on all or most major assignments and objectives.

2 Performance is inconsistent; meets some job requirements but not consistently. Overall performance is below the acceptable level and must improve to meet minimum position requirements.

1 Performance is consistently below job requirements. Fails to meet position requirements in most areas. A corrective action plan and performance improvement are mandatory.

NA/NO This accountability is not applicable or has not been observed by the reviewer.

(continued)

Example 3 *(continued)*

Job Area	Remarks	Rating
1. **Professional Knowledge/Work Knowledge/Skills:** Possesses and applies knowledge or skills necessary for task completion. Keeps current on new developments in area of work.	Knowledge exceeds what is required to perform well.	4
2. **Quality of Work:** Assignments are accurate, complete, and comply with objectives.	Performs efficiently and well.	3
3. **Quantity of Work:** Produces significant volume of work to support goals within specified time frames.	Work is regularly completed on time and error free.	3
4. **Communication:** Maintains open, effective communications with all employees and clients. Written and verbal communications are clear, concise, and understandable.	Can explain complicated procedures well. Can express herself clearly in written communication.	4
5. **Teamwork:** Willingly cooperates, shares information, assists, and is tolerant of others in daily interaction with all employees, vendors, and clients.	Gets along well with fellow team members.	3
6. **Reliability:** Can be relied on to complete tasks and follow up as needed.	Does not disappoint when deadlines are tight.	4
7. **Adaptability/Flexibility:** Easily adjusts to changes in routine, assignments, and company/client needs and continues to be productive.	Willingly assumes others' tasks in case of absences.	5
8. **Initiative:** Voluntarily recommends resourceful, alternative, or original ideas/procedures for work improvement or problem solution.	Will take risks to accommodate customers. Instituted extranet connection for vendor **X** to improve project coordination.	4
9. **Planning/Scheduling:** Prioritizes tasks, anticipates needs, and makes adjustments.	Others regularly rely on her scheduling abilities.	5
10. **Problem Solving:** Identifies problems within own area, develops resourceful solutions, and makes recommendations for corrective action.	Thorough in analyzing and developing solutions.	4

Example 3 *(continued)*

Summary

Sections 1, 2, 3, and 4 should be completed by the supervisor. Section 5 should be completed by the employee.

1. Major accomplishments since last review

2. Job-related strengths

3. Areas for improvement/development

4. Action plan

5. Employee comments

Signatures

I acknowledge that this review has been discussed with me. My signature does not imply agreement or disagreement.

Employee: Date:

Supervisor: Date:

Human Resources: Date:

Part Three

Perfect Phrases for Performance Reviews

Accuracy

Outstanding

- Maintains high accuracy under tight deadlines
- Catches virtually all mistakes before submitting final work
- Achieves zero errors when required
- Trusted to do tasks demanding high accuracy
- Less than 1 percent error rate
- Helps others improve their accuracy

Exceeds Expectations

- Takes pride in accuracy
- Looks to improve continuously by learning
- Maintains accuracy even under pressure
- Managers have commented on high level of accuracy
- Identifies own errors early on
- Exceeds part-tolerance standards
- Customers have commented on her precision and attention to detail

Meets Expectations

- Checks finished product before forwarding
- Uses technical tools to improve accuracy (for example, spell-checker)
- Does not require constant supervision
- Balances accuracy with speed
- Produces 99.9 percent of parts within specifications
- Accuracy rates are comparable to those of colleagues

Needs Improvement

- Sometimes makes small errors
- Tends to overlook details
- Less than 5 percent errors but more than 2 percent
- Desire to be perfect slows down production
- Tends to miss small mistakes

- Commits more errors than others in similar position
- More than 2 percent of parts made need to be scrapped
- Colleagues or peers need to rework his/her output to fix

Unacceptable
- Does not check work before submitting
- Errors have caused money loss
- Mistakes have caused customer loss
- Error rate over ___ percent
- ___ customers have complained about errors
- Misses small and large mistakes
- Accuracy has not improved despite 10 hours of retraining
- Over 5 percent of product output not to specification
- Accuracy poor enough to cause safety concerns

Self-Monitoring/Self-Evaluation
- Can you think of some situations where you demonstrated the ability to maintain your accuracy under time pressures?
- Were there any times where you felt that you were less accurate in your [insert function] than at other times? What do you think caused that?
- What things/events interfered with your ability to check your work before sending it on or otherwise interfered with your accuracy when you [insert function]?

Looking Forward
- Is there any training or learning you could use to go from acceptable accuracy to outstanding accuracy according to our criteria?
- What can I do as your supervisor to help you cut your error rate from 3 percent down to 1 percent?
- What do you feel you need to do to get your error rates equal to or better than those of your colleagues?
- You are so accurate in all of your work, can you think of ways you could help your coworkers achieve the same degree of accuracy?

Administrative Skills

Outstanding

- Has improved many departmental procedures
- Effectively tracks the status of projects
- Handles many tasks simultaneously
- Documents are always ready when needed
- Created important new record keeping systems
- Has helped coworkers become more organized
- Is the go-to person when anyone needs to have policies or procedures explained
- Runs the office even though it's not a formal responsibility
- Keeps others on task to get work done
- Examines, questions, and improves administrative procedures
- Has generated more than two cost-savings administrative procedure improvements during the last year

Exceeds Expectations

- Streamlined many procedures
- Administers accounts payable and receivable without error
- Administers many functions without error
- Thorough, reliable, and accurate
- Maintains vital information
- Sets priorities well
- Steps up to help organize things even when it's not his job
- Almost never unable to find files/papers/resources/books
- Has taken on administrative tasks to relieve load on manager
- Has exerted positive influence on staff to get time and expense sheets in on time
- Shows creativity in finding better solutions that fit the bill

Meets Expectations

- Files and finds documents in a timely fashion
- Consistently demonstrates administrative skills required

- Maintains important records on time and with acceptable accuracy
- Writes clear memos
- Sets priorities to ensure documents are ready when needed
- Uses project management software effectively
- Takes and distributes meeting minutes in a timely and accurate fashion as requested
- Follows administrative procedures precisely

Needs Improvement
- Sometimes follows procedures too rigidly
- Has lost or temporarily misplaced important data in past year
- Had difficulty using a filing system others can follow and understand
- Not always open to suggestions about how to be more efficient
- Some records can't be found or are inaccurate
- Sometimes does not maintain records
- Reports are lost on occasion
- Administration is a weakness
- Cannot create graphs
- Rarely relies on the computer to simplify tasks
- Makes grammatical and punctuation errors in memos

Unacceptable
- Refuses to use new software tools supplied
- Administrative tasks often late
- Has slowed down other staff by not completing administrative responsibilities on time
- Administrative skills have not improved despite supervisory coaching
- Memos/other written work products often unclear
- Slow to volunteer during crunch times
- Reports are often misfiled and lost
- Has missed a number of important deadlines
- Several sales lost due to slowness, disorganization

Self-Monitoring/Self-Evaluation

- Over the past year, how have you created good cooperative relationships with the rest of the office so you can do your job well?
- Would you like us to change any procedures or rules so you can administer the program/office more efficiently?
- In what performance areas do you feel you need significant improvement?
- Describe to me a situation where you applied your administrative skills in a way that was above and beyond the call of duty?

Looking Forward

- Have you come across any software or similar affordable tools that you feel would make the organizing part of your job easier and more effective?
- Is there any training you feel would be instrumental in pushing your performance even higher?
- Do you feel that you might benefit if we spend a half hour a week discussing some of the challenges of the previous week and how you could have addressed them?

Analytic Skills

Outstanding
- Demonstrated ability to analyze a situation, plan a solution, and implement effectively
- Can zero in on the root cause of a problem
- Not led astray by superficial causes of problems
- Can perceive relationships in a mass of data
- Excellent analyst
- Translates analysis into appropriate actions
- Communicates analysis results clearly and concisely

Exceeds Expectations
- Possesses above average analytic skills
- Analysis shows insight
- Methodical analyst
- In six production failures, made a diagnosis and repair within two hours
- Clearly communicates analysis results to others
- Often identifies issues coworkers have missed
- Demonstrates understanding of logical errors and never makes them

Meets Expectations
- Detail oriented without losing sight of the bigger picture
- Possesses the skills to solve basic on-the-job problems
- Analyzes data and makes appropriate recommendations
- Summarizes reports from five supervisors in time for Monday managers' meetings
- Possesses sufficient statistical skills to properly interpret data

Needs Improvement
- Needs to develop skills to analyze situations
- Frequently draws wrong conclusions from data
- Understands data well but fails to take into account human factors in analysis

- Analysis tends to stop short and misses some details
- Analysis sometimes focuses on the unimportant
- Places too much trust in the opinions of others about data
- Takes too many shortcuts to save time and effort
- Analytic results are questioned by others and found wanting
- Makes mathematical/calculation errors
- Errors caused problems in 3 out of 10 instances

Unacceptable
- Analysis is limited to superficial elements only
- At least one instance where inadequate analysis cost company money or clients
- Makes analytic errors regularly
- Must rely on others to calculate and interpret statistical data
- Analytic skills are below what's necessary
- Frequently comes to inaccurate conclusions
- Was unable to solve problems for 3 out of 10 customers on help line
- Refuses to accept responsibility when analysis or conclusions are wrong

Self-Monitoring/Self-Evaluation
- What analytic approaches have you used that have worked really well for you in the last year and that you should continue using?
- Are there any analytic methods that did not work well during the last year?
- In terms of last year's projects you were involved with, what would you do differently in terms of diagnosis and analysis of problems?
- How often do you feel it took you too long to identify the root problem?

Looking Forward
- If there's an opportunity for some professional development

next year, are there any conferences or courses you feel would help you learn or hone your analysis skills?

- Would you like more one-on-one time with me so we can talk about your thinking and conclusions on projects?
- In the coming year, in terms of mistakes or approaches, what do you want to avoid regarding your problem-solving and analysis tasks?

Appraisal and Evaluation Skills

Outstanding

- Conscientiously gathers information to fairly appraise employees
- Able to individualize conversations with staff to take into account what works best
- Works cooperatively with staff in appraisals
- Uses appraisal to build commitment and motivation
- Provides substantial documentation of performance
- Conducts appraisals on time
- Bases appraisal on pre-agreed goals
- Negotiates fair and appropriate goals
- Negotiates stretch goals to help employees improve
- Encourages self-evaluation and gives credence to employee self-evaluation
- Aligns strategic planning, unit planning, and employee goal setting
- Uses past experience to improve future performance
- Can fairly assess how he/she contributed to any performance problems

Exceeds Expectations

- Puts employees at ease
- Properly explains purpose of appraisal and evaluation system
- Gains employees' commitment to performance improvement
- Gets staff involved as partners in the appraisal process
- Evaluations seem free from bias
- Performance- and results-focused
- Creates positive, developmental-focused tone
- Explains appraisal process clearly
- Prepares documents prior to each appraisal
- Negotiates goals
- Uses appraisals to achieve departmental goals

Meets Expectations

- Understands biases that can interfere with evaluation
- Handles appraisal responsibilities well
- Believes in the importance of appraisal
- Appraises job performance fairly
- Develops employees with appraisal process
- Involves employees in setting goals
- Records employees' reactions
- Documents significant employee behaviors
- Regularly communicates with employees about performance

Needs Improvement

- Noticeably uncomfortable with appraisals
- Doesn't listen or acknowledge employee concerns
- Discounts employee self-evaluations
- Defensive when challenged by employees on evaluations
- Critical toward employees, not developmental
- Focuses on past and blame, not future
- Determines goals without employee input
- Appraisal discussions are one-sided
- Employees regularly disagree with appraisals
- Employees complain appraisals are not adequately prepared
- Rubber-stamps employee self-evaluations without discussion
- Just wants to get the form off his desk
- Appears not to understand how to use the performance appraisal tools
- Does not understand why performance appraisal is important or how it can help employees and managers
- Communicates with employees about performance only once a year
- Often surprises employees with the comments/evaluations made during the once-a-year appraisals
- Completes forms but seems unable to follow "spirit" of the appraisal process
- Stops doing appraisals when employee hits top of pay range

Unacceptable

- Portrays evaluations as "a joke" or "waste of time" in front of staff
- Has no understanding of his/her own possible biases
- Produces rating influenced by most recent events rather than entire year without a reason
- Biased ratings influenced by personal friendships
- Does not set clear goals at beginning of appraisal period
- Appraisal documents are frequently late
- HR has to nag to get properly completed appraisals
- Does not involve staff in appraisal process
- Rather than negotiating, dictates goals to staff members
- Makes many rating errors
- Spends only _____ minutes on appraisal

Self-Monitoring/Self-Evaluation

- What kinds of circumstances generally have caused the delays in discussing performance with your employees?
- If we asked your staff about how useful the appraisals are, what do you think their opinions would be?
- Are there any areas of the performance management process that could use improvement?

Looking Forward

- You and I meet regularly to discuss your performance. What can you do to improve the process with your employees since It's a job requirement?
- If you would like some help conducting the appraisal meetings with your staff, I'd be glad to help you so you'll be more comfortable and get them done.
- Since the quality of the appraisals you 've been doing seem problematic, and several employees have commented negatively, I think next year we'll do some of them together, so I can help out.

Attitude or Approach to Work

Outstanding

- Cordial and happy to help
- Looks for ways to help others
- Always upbeat and optimistic
- Views success in relation to group's success
- Enthusiastic and energetic
- Quick to volunteer even for tough tasks
- Inspires others to exhibit positive work attitude

Exceeds Expectations

- Deals positively with setbacks
- Tactful when communicating about problems
- Direct, straightforward, and honest
- Doesn't blame problems on others
- Always takes responsibility for own behavior
- Eager for feedback from others
- Always pleasant to be around
- Often gives credit for accomplishments to other team members
- Leads others by example—great role model

Meets Expectations

- Rarely down
- Polite and civil to coworkers
- Has received no verified complaints about interpersonal conduct (from peers)
- Cooperative and cordial
- Always focuses on getting things done
- Volunteered to be a member of the Worklife Committee
- Has can-do attitude

Needs Improvement

- Has been involved with coworker conflicts that required third-party mediation

- When stressed, tone can be overly aggressive and off-putting to peers
- Can be quarrelsome
- Tends to assign blame rather than prevent problem from happening again
- Can be negative
- Projects "in it for myself" attitude
- Rarely helps others
- Seems absent and uninterested at team meetings
- Needs to be prompted to stop daydreaming
- Coworkers refuse to contribute because of her harsh comments

Unacceptable

- Negatively affects coworkers due to lack of common courtesy
- Refuses to learn or be coached
- Can be snobbish, often sounds arrogant
- Presents a facade of infallibility but is often wrong
- Flaunts academic degrees to demonstrate superiority; turns off other employees
- Presence often creates tension in group
- Not cooperative
- Frequently criticizes others
- Pessimistic
- Always finding fault with others
- Has been involved in more than one public shouting match at work
- Coworkers have indicated they don't like to work with this person

Self-Monitoring/Self-Evaluation

- How do you think your coworkers see you—as an upbeat positive person, a negative person, or somewhere in the middle?
- On the comment cards we receive from customers, what do you think your average rating is on "courtesy"? And why do you think you received that rating?

- I've noticed that you tend to be more critical of ideas than the other staff. How do you think that affects how others feel about coming to work?
- What is your biggest strength and biggest weakness in terms of contributing to the positive atmosphere here?

Looking Forward

- I know you are going through a lot personally. Is there anything that can be done to prevent the personal things affecting you from negatively affecting your work?
- I noticed that you and John don't get along very well and you seem to dislike him. Since you need to work together, we need to come up with a plan to make that workable.
- If you and John have a problem, I'd be glad to discuss it with both of you with a no-blame approach so we can make it easier for everyone to get along.
- Is there anything you can do to improve your ability to get along with coworkers?

Coaching

Outstanding
- Coaches others without being asked
- A role model, teacher, and guide
- Identifies weaknesses and solutions without being pushy
- Inspires others to do better
- Outstanding ability to explain and teach
- Helps others identify their strengths and weaknesses
- Always finds time to answer work questions of employees

Exceeds Expectations
- Builds independent thinking in others
- Strongly supports others' attempts at improvement
- Excellent at demonstrating appropriate procedures
- Delivers feedback directly and constructively
- Applauds effort
- Takes new employees "under her wing"
- Employees have expressed appreciation for the help given

Meets Expectations
- Times coaching interventions effectively
- Does not overwhelm other person
- Draws out knowledge and skills from others
- Leads people to discover their own answers
- Available when needed
- Allocates time for the coaching process

Needs Improvement
- Isn't effective with people slow to learn
- Guides and coaches, but doesn't let others have responsibility
- Gets frustrated when others aren't learning
- Assumes too much knowledge on others' part
- Doesn't enable staff to reduce dependency
- Has difficulty integrating coaching with rest of job

Unacceptable

- Dictates to others rather than involving them
- Slow to delegate authority as employee learns
- Insensitive to needs of other people
- Has reduced another person to tears on at least one occasion
- Staff uncomfortable being coached by him/her
- Believes coaching not part of her job
- Strong dislike of working with others is apparent
- Overbearing in coaching interactions
- Has had several emotional blowups during coaching sessions
- Several employees refuse to be coached by this person

Self-Monitoring/Self-Evaluation

- Do you feel you have an aptitude for coaching and helping others at work?
- We all have weaknesses and strengths. Could you tell me what your strengths are that make you a good coach?
- I'm asking staff who coach employees to complete a short checklist right after the coaching sessions, so they can identify their own coaching patterns. I'd like you to do that too, and we'll go over them once a month.
- If there was one thing you could change about yourself to make yourself a better coach, what would it be?

Looking Forward

- We're bringing in some books and videos on the coaching process so all our managers can access them as needed. I'd like each manager to spend an hour a month learning about coaching.
- Bernice is really good at coaching others. Since you are relatively new to coaching employees, I'd like you to pair up and observe how she works in those situations.
- It's important for people coaching others to learn continuously, so I'd like you to identify some resources you think would help make you a better coach, and we'll see what the budget allows.

Communication Skills: Verbal

Outstanding

- Superior skills on phone and in meetings
- Speaks persuasively and convincingly
- Thoughtful and responsive to employees at all levels
- Is an articulate spokesperson for the team's views
- Interacts with audience
- Develops clear, concise computer presentations
- Admits when he doesn't know rather than "faking it"
- Has received at least two positive comments about how clear her explanations are
- Has the knack of making anyone she talks to feel special and heard

Exceeds Expectations

- Is convincing and confident when speaking
- Prepares properly for all important communications
- Speaks articulately and concisely
- Adept at technical explanations
- Concludes on an upbeat note
- Answers questions directly
- Solves customer problems faster than average due to ability to give clear explanations
- Frequently seeks out feedback on how he communicates
- Knows when to slow down when speaking so listeners can absorb what has been said

Meets Expectations

- Uses collateral material effectively
- Can explain complicated procedures well
- Rarely fumbles for an answer
- Knows where to find answers if he doesn't know
- Seems comfortable while presenting
- Articulate and well-organized speaker

- Clear, understandable voice
- Used technology effectively when speaking to a group
- Speaks at speed appropriate so others understand

Needs Improvement

- Speaks in monotone
- Is not confident when presenting
- Reads script and has little contact with audience
- Uncomfortable responding to questions
- Makes occasional grammatical mistakes when speaking
- Positions often not clearly thought out
- Occasionally loses the thread of what she is trying to say
- Poor enunciation and mumbling causes listeners to be frustrated
- Uses too many PowerPoint slides in business presentations

Unacceptable

- Often makes grammatical errors when speaking that affect credibility
- Does not build rapport when speaking with others
- Does not build audience participation when needed
- Often misunderstands what others are saying, leading to mistakes on the job
- Does not know how to ask questions that will guide work
- Has had to be rescued by others during group presentations because she confused the audience
- Uses unacceptable language and/or jokes when speaking
- Unprofessional demeanor in groups

Self-Monitoring/Self-Evaluation

- How would you evaluate the presentations you've made to customer groups during the past year?
- We don't tend to think about how we communicate one-on-one in the office, but we all should. Give me an example of how you have communicated clearly.

- When you had the chance to take that course in verbal communication, what are the most important things you learned and applied on your job?
- Who is your favorite "communicator" and what do you like best about him/her that you'd like to incorporate into your own style of communicating?

Looking Forward

- Communication is so important for all of us in these jobs, so I'd like you to spend a little time thinking about a self-development plan for improving your verbal communication. Then we'll see what is practical.
- All of us could be better at communicating with our customers. How would you feel about attending a communication skills training session sometime this year?
- Would you be willing to have me or someone else give you feedback on how you communicate with the clients?

Communication Skills: Written

Outstanding

- Exceptional communicator
- All writing (final copies) free of punctuation or grammatical errors
- Clear, concise, error-free writing
- Excellent at persuasive writing
- Wrote bids that gained business 7 out of 10 times
- Best proposal writer on staff based on acceptance rates
- Regularly receives positive feedback on clarity of writing
- Able to tailor message to address needs of the specific customer
- Writes well under deadline pressure without loss of quality

Exceeds Expectations

- Written communications easily understood
- Writes quickly, clearly, and correctly
- Consults references when unsure of proper spelling, punctuation, or grammar
- Uses formatting effectively to highlight key information
- Documentation is consistently understood
- Translations of documentation were free of confusion
- E-mails and memos are clear and to the point

Meets Expectations

- Can express herself clearly in written communication
- Competent writer
- Makes few grammar or punctuation errors
- Spelling usually correct
- Conveys information reasonably clearly
- Writes professional communications, including e-mail
- Uses language at appropriate difficulty level of potential readers
- Rereads e-mails and memos before sending to ensure proper emotional tone

Needs Improvement

- The point of written communications not always clear
- Tends to ramble in written communications in a way that confuses readers
- Makes grammatical and punctuation errors in copy he submits
- Takes a long time to get to the point
- Provides too much detail and clouds the critical issues as a result
- Written communications sometimes lead to misunderstandings
- Many people were confused about report X
- Customers have to phone for clarification of points in the reports she writes
- Occasionally leaves out important points needed for readers to understand the issues
- Written communication too bureaucratic
- Uses jargon and abbreviations without explaining them properly
- Assumes too much basic knowledge on the part of the reader

Unacceptable

- Poor writer who hasn't improved despite feedback over last year
- Numerous errors and lack of organization make understanding difficult
- Credibility of employee and company damaged by comments and jokes in written material
- Writing fails to meet company standards
- Writing represents our company poorly
- Many customers failed to understand the August Bulletin
- Poor written communication resulted in errors costing $___
- Has sent inappropriate e-mails at least three times in last year to coworkers

Self-Monitoring/Self-Evaluation

- I know I sometimes have trouble with grammar when I'm writing. Do you feel you have a good grasp of grammar to write properly constructed reports?

- What methods do you use to ensure that the reports you submit are free of spelling and grammatical mistakes?

- Do you feel your readers/customers see you as a credible resource based on your written communication? What specifically do you think enhances your credibility when you write?

Looking Forward

- Let's sit down and look at some ways you can improve the organization of the proposals you write.

- Since the proposals we send to customers are the lifeblood of our business, about once a year, I'd like you to submit a proposal you think is really good and one that is less effective so we can talk about what works.

- I hope to bring in an expert to help us with our reports and proposals, so if there are any writing issues (grammar, structuring, etc.) that you'd like to learn about, please submit them to me.

Computer Skills: Regular Maintenance and Security

Outstanding

- Assists others who are having trouble maintaining their machines by themselves
- Almost never calls outside technical help since he does basic software and system maintenance on his own
- Leads and encourages others to practice safe computing

Exceeds Expectations

- Calls for help are less frequent than the average for his peers
- Is alert for security problems across the network, not just on his own machine
- Her computers are kept clean and clear from debris and blockages to airflow
- Handles most routine updates and maintenance on her own
- Has never had a virus on his computer

Meets Expectations

- Backs up laptop as mandated per company policy and stores backups in company secure facility on time
- Follows guidelines and policies for keeping data secure
- Attempts to solve basic computer problems before calling in expensive help
- Uses proper security procedures to protect company data on laptop
- Properly ensures physical security of computer in his care
- Does not leave computer while logged in and makes sure to log out when absent from desk

Needs Improvement

- Does not do backups on schedule
- Is impatient and easily frustrated when his machines do not work properly

- Unable to describe issues and problems with the machines he uses to help information technician
- Has been observed eating and/or drinking over the keyboards in our data room
- Tends to leave her computer without logging out, allowing anyone to use the computer under her account
- Does not follow policy about using proper complex passwords

Unacceptable

- Twice has introduced a virus to the network by using unauthorized software
- Makes significantly more requests for computer maintenance help to the IT department than any other employee
- Has taken confidential company information out of the office
- Has twice lost important information by not backing up his laptop properly
- Has twice lost company computer hardware while out of the office
- Routinely circumvents company security by using proxy servers at work to access unacceptable sites
- Disables antivirus programs installed on machines he uses
- Has had pirated software on company machines

Self-Monitoring/Self-Evaluation

- So you won't forget any steps, please write up a checklist to ensure that data on your laptop is protected.
- What steps can you take to make sure we don't have a repeat of the computer virus infestation of last year?
- Tell me about a time when you forgot to follow security practices for the computers you use.

Looking Forward

- You need to safeguard the data in your care. Are the procedures for doing so clear?

- I'd like you to help other employees learn and apply safe computing practices in the office. Can you pull together a few ideas that would help?
- Let's go over the password procedure you use for both your work computer and your personal computer to make sure you have maximum security.

Computer Skills: Software Purchasing and Selection

Outstanding

- Consults with and involves all users in software choices
- Her software selection has been excellent with users having only minor complaints about its usability
- Has balanced features vs. price to ensure software choices meet organization needs without unnecessary expenditures
- Grasp of both business needs and requirements plus technical knowledge means we can trust her to make software choices on her own

Exceeds Expectations

- Understands the "best" software is that which fits *our* needs
- Separates advertising hype from facts and is not unduly influenced by popularity
- Always considers support availability for products before purchasing
- Meticulous and detail-oriented when purchasing software on behalf of company or recommending a specific purchase

Meets Expectations

- Follows best practices in selecting software
- Does adequate research on the technical advantages and disadvantages of competing software packages
- Consults other users to identify their needs and concerns
- Other users have generally been happy with the software he has purchased for the company

Needs Improvement

- Tends to be swayed by what is popular rather than our own company needs
- Does not take into account availability of internal support and knowledge for software packages resulting in expensive retraining for IT/help desk staff

- Tends to want to purchase software that is more complex than necessary
- Does not always take into account what our future business needs might involve

Unacceptable

- Does not consult end users before software selection and purchase
- Users have been disappointed and frustrated when software he purchased was overly complex or lacked critical features
- Has cost the company significant amounts of money by choosing poorly supported or inadequate software
- Does minimal research and makes choices based on gut feeling
- Required retraining in basics of systems analysis to hone software review skills

Self-Monitoring/Self-Evaluation

- Generally speaking, how do you feel your selection of software tools has served the intended purpose?
- How have other users reacted to your choice of software tools?

Looking Forward

- What changes can you make in the future to avoid software purchases that are seen as problematic by other users?
- What have you learned about software purchasing that will help you improve your purchases in the future?
- Can you research some professional development options so you can hone your software selection skills?
- For the next round of software purchases, I'd like to be more involved so I can help you define the business needs of our unit.

Computer Skills: Social Media Use

Outstanding

- Has acquired incredible skills in tweaking our Facebook pages and making our pages stand out
- Very effective in monitoring social media for mentions of our company name for business intelligence purposes
- Has mastered social media for both marketing/sales media and provided after-sales follow-up
- Has been recognized by a third party as an example of someone using social media effectively

Exceeds Expectations

- Intervenes early when he finds negative references to our company on blogs, Twitter, and Facebook
- Able to turn around a higher-than-average percentage of irate customers on social media
- Is a credible source of information about our company and projects our high standards to the public
- Repeatedly remained calm and in control in the face of personal insults made online
- Freely shares his expertise with others to create more in-house experts

Meets Expectations

- Drafts effective communications regarding sales/benefits on Facebook and other platforms
- Blogs regularly on corporate blog
- Responds to customer questions on blog within one working day
- Responses to customer complaints are calm and constructive
- Treats online customers fairly and equitably
- Stays within the limits and guidelines in terms of making restitution to angry customers

Needs Improvement

- Has difficulties expressing himself within 140-character limit, which interferes on occasion with customer communication
- Sometimes she forgets she's representing the company and not just herself
- Occasionally makes mistakes interpreting what customers are saying, and doesn't verify her understanding enough
- Has made promises on behalf of the company that cannot be kept
- Has made public derogatory remarks about competitor's products and service

Unacceptable

- Has used inappropriate language with abusive customers on social media platforms
- Has made his own negative comments about the company in public Internet spaces
- Errs on the side of being suspicious of customers and has accused online customers of lying
- Far too reactive to represent the company without constant supervision
- Uses same identity for personal and corporate social media use, confusing possible customers

Self-Monitoring/Self-Evaluation

- How do you feel about the rate of business growth you are generating through Facebook and Twitter?
- How do you feel the social media initiative you are involved in is paying off for the company?
- Do you think the time you spend on social media is well justified? How could you be allocating your time differently?

Looking Forward

- How has your understanding of social media improved?

- What do you need to become more expert during the coming year?
- Are there any learning resources we can get you to help you keep up with all the changes within social media?
- What single aspect of working with social media would you like to improve in?

Computer Skills: Training Others

Outstanding

- Excellent tutor and coach of others to help them become more proficient at the computer
- Often better at teaching others how to be more efficient on the computer than the regular IT software trainers
- Has compiled job aids to assist others in developing their computer skills
- Shows patience and understanding when coaching others to use our in-house software
- Takes the initiative to keep up with latest computer software on her own time

Exceeds Expectations

- Almost always available to help when a coworker gets stuck with a computer problem
- Has cut our wait time and downtime by 20 percent for software assistance by helping out
- When she doesn't have the answer to a computer issue, knows where to get the information
- When training others in small groups, makes sure everyone understands before moving to the next topic

Meets Expectations

- Always willing to help with computer issues, even though it's not his job
- Communicates highly technical topics in plain language so others can understand
- Keeps up with new technology sufficiently to help others

Needs Improvement

- Sometimes uses computer jargon when it is unnecessary or easily understood
- Gets impatient with slower learners in group settings
- Has difficulty realizing when his information is outdated

- Does not always teach in efficient, logical ways
- Forgets what is easy for him is not necessarily easy for others
- Has not had enough exposure to adult learning principles to teach effectively

Unacceptable

- Has raised voice in frustration several times during computer training sessions
- Other staff do not like her to be in charge of their training
- Is incomplete in the information he teaches to others
- Pays insufficient attention to detail when training others
- Often interrupts the IT staff when they lead group training

Self-Monitoring/Self-Evaluation

- When you train others on the computer, how do you know that they understand what you're telling them?
- What single thing could you do to be more effective instructing others on using the computer?
- If we asked people you have trained to use the computer system about your training skills, what do you think would be your best qualities and your least satisfactory?
- Are there areas where you can improve as a computer trainer?

Looking Forward

- What courses would help you become a more valuable computer trainer?
- What single thing would you like to change in terms of helping others learn effective computer use?
- Your background is more on the technical side than the training/learning side. What could we do to upgrade your one-to-one training skills?
- I'd like you to sit in on Mark Davis's Introduction to [product name] so you can see how he does it. Mark is really good, so let's schedule a day or two, and then we'll sit down with Mark and discuss what works.

Outstanding

- Has mastered the use of the major tools we use on a day-to-day basis (Excel, Word, MySQL)
- Quickly solves all software and hardware problems
- Has championed movement to paperless operations
- Designed, implemented, and manages department's intranet site
- Creates forms that are virtually foolproof
- Produced ___ documents with only ___ requiring rework
- Conducted ___ Internet searches, with only ___ research queries requiring additional information
- Able to choose the right software tool for the job almost every time
- Uses software features to find the fastest way to do tasks

Exceeds Expectations

- Demonstrates ability to use search engines to do corporate research online
- Has strengths in many of our regularly used programs
- Helps others with advanced computer function questions
- Established many protocols for electronic file keeping
- Quickly learns new programs
- Finds customer records quickly while on the phone using our database system
- Formatted ___-page document within ___ days from receipt of submissions
- Created database with ___ fields (___ relational) in ___days
- Redesigned enterprise system to speed processing without affecting users

Meets Expectations

- Competent with all software used
- Can fix minor hardware problems

- Effectively communicates expectations to IT personnel
- Understands Windows basics
- Handles computer problems without getting frustrated
- With the exception of program X, keeps up with colleagues
- Entered _____ customer delivery requests with _____ errors

Needs Improvement
- Resists updating her skills when software is upgraded
- Has difficulty with essential programs
- Makes repeated formatting errors
- Learning new software is a challenge
- Sometimes forgets to turn off computer
- Can't find saved files
- Loaded personal software against policy
- Caused two major system failures

Unacceptable
- Lacks the computer skills this job requires
- Makes repeated errors after repeated instructions
- Has not learned basics
- After six months still has problems finding customer records
- Asks questions found in help file
- Calls help desk frequently
- Doesn't heed warning messages
- Deleted required software in error

Self-Monitoring/Self-Evaluation
- In what specific areas do you need to upgrade skills to use the computer effectively?
- What kinds of hardware or software problems have you encountered that negatively affect your efficient use of the computer?
- Please describe the company's personal use policies we have for company computers.
- How often are you stumped and need help from others to use the software for your job?

- Which software package causes you the most difficulty?
- How do you react when you can't get the computer to do what you need?

Looking Forward

- Do you need to refresh your knowledge about the XYZ software package in the next year?
- How do you think you could better keep up with all the new developments with our in-house software?
- I rely on you to tell me about the latest things coming down the pike in terms of software. I'd like that to be part of your job. Let's plan to meet every month to talk about it.

Conflict Management

Outstanding

- Has resolved several difficult conflicts this year
- Avoids conflict escalation
- Received customer compliments for resolving a conflict through calm negotiation
- Made partners out of enemies
- Acts as conflict troubleshooter within organization
- Is involved in personal conflicts far less than any other staff member
- Knows how to analyze a conflict to determine whether it's worth addressing directly

Exceeds Expectations

- Looks for common ground
- Listens carefully to both sides
- Builds customer loyalty through conflict management
- Diplomatic without sidestepping critical issues
- Peers seek his/her advice in dealing with conflict situations
- Understands when compromise is needed
- Remains calm and considerate even when everyone is stressed and snippy
- Knows when it is appropriate to give in and when to continue pushing for his solution

Meets Expectations

- Uses basic mediation techniques as fits the situation
- Uses outside personnel when necessary
- Handles conflict in calm, unemotional ways
- Remains calm in tough situations
- Effective third party in handling disputes
- Knows when he is overmatched in a conflict situation

Needs Improvement

- Sometimes impatient with disagreement
- Becomes defensive in some conflicts
- Has an ongoing conflict with another staff member
- Starts unnecessary conflict when stressed
- Superiors sometimes need to step in
- Has said things in anger that have damaged his relationships with colleagues

Unacceptable

- Has made several conflicts worse
- Will not yield in conflict
- Rarely makes compromises
- Argues for trivial reasons
- Often focuses on blaming others
- Does not recognize when outside help needed
- Attitude a primary cause of conflict with other people

Self-Monitoring/Self-Evaluation

- Give me an example of when your coworkers came to you to help them manage conflict.
- Specifically what causes the conflicts you have with Tom?
- What do you need to change to handle coworker conflicts more effectively?
- What causes conflicts with customers?
- What is your greatest strength when dealing with frustrated customers?
- How is stress a factor in your patience with coworkers or conflicts?
- How can you better choose the right conflict management strategy to fit the situation?

Looking Forward

- Would you feel comfortable talking to Employee Assistance about your stress and conflict levels?

- Let's see if we can create an action plan for you to help reduce conflicts. What's the first thing you feel you would need to change?
- I'd like to see you cut down instances of serious conflict with your colleagues. What help can I offer so we can make this happen?

Cooperation

Outstanding

- Does everything asked without objection
- Immediately puts clients' requests above other work
- Works in concert with others
- Unrivaled willingness to help
- Understands and acts on principle that team players help each other succeed
- Establishes rapport with everyone
- Works on four project teams, volunteers on two others

Exceeds Expectations

- Always asks others if he can help if he has extra time
- Shares ideas freely
- Will do what it takes to work with others
- Effective representative of department
- Works toward team goals without consideration of personal effect
- Formed team with representatives from departments affected by software program X
- Other staff often ask to work with her because of her positive attitude

Meets Expectations

- Works well with other departments
- Puts good of company above that of department
- Is flexible with priorities
- Willing to cooperate
- Sensitive to others' needs without sacrificing own work
- Received compliments on spirit of cooperation on the XYZ project

Needs Improvement

- Will object to work when it interferes with schedule
- Is often reluctant to help others on the job

- Won't bend on views without coercion
- Shows lack of cooperation on team projects
- Declined an offer to be part of XYZ team
- Often rigid on matters like scheduling, work responsibilities

Unacceptable

- Argues with team members over petty issues
- Will not change views
- Inflexible and noncompliant
- Refused to follow rules during a spill cleanup
- Consistently neglects regulation to mark hazardous waste
- When working as part of team, she often argues about who does what
- Spends time worrying about what others are and are not doing, rather than doing his job

Self-Monitoring/Self-Evaluation

- What is your greatest strength in working cooperatively with customers? What about a weakness?
- Do you think of yourself as flexible, strongly opinionated, or maybe a little of both? Why?
- What situations have arisen with coworkers where you feel you weren't getting the cooperation you hoped for?
- Do you prefer to work side by side with others or do you prefer to work on your own? Why?
- Describe a time when you felt taken advantage of by your colleagues.

Looking Forward

- We need you to be more flexible and open to the ideas of your coworkers. How can we get there?
- You need to cooperate better with other departments in terms of following their procedures. How can you achieve that?
- In our team meetings, what mannerisms might you change so you seem less frustrated?

Cost Cutting

Outstanding

- Exceeded cost-cutting targets this year
- Developed innovative cost-cutting measures
- Improved profit margin by ___ percent last year
- Developed company-wide cost-cutting suggestion program
- Saved six jobs in his department by finding ways to cut waste
- Demonstrated ability to use statistical techniques to identify areas where efficiency could be improved
- Led the way in salary cuts by agreeing to take 20 percent less when only required to drop by 10 percent

Exceeds Expectations

- Developed methods to identify cost overruns
- Asks for cost-cutting suggestions from staff
- Used techniques (e.g., outsourcing) effectively
- Welcomes and evaluates any cost-cutting ideas
- Has worked diligently to increase productivity of staff through coaching so new staff are not needed despite workloads

Meets Expectations

- Implemented corporate strategies
- Met cost-cutting goals
- Stays within budgeted guidelines
- Maintained productivity along with modest cost savings
- Is frugal with company funds
- Gets the most out of existing physical resources and tools by ensuring they are properly maintained so replacement costs are lowered

Needs Improvement

- Sacrificed productivity by cutting too deep
- Insists on spending budget even if not needed

- Needs to improve methods for priority spending
- Has taken advantage of perks on travel status
- Continues to allow himself unnecessary luxuries while staff go without

Unacceptable

- Cost-cutting measures backfired, department crippled
- Unit unable to function properly
- Spends with no reflection or prioritization
- Supervisors need to scrutinize every expenditure
- Pads expenses

Self-Monitoring/Self-Evaluation

- How do you look for ways to lower our expenses when you are on the road?
- Are there any more ways you can think of to be more productive with the same resources?
- During the last year you ordered a number of books and other materials. What did you find most useful and least useful?
- During the last year we were asked to cut our expenditures by 10 percent. How did you do in that respect?
- Have you identified any other areas we haven't yet talked about to reduce our costs of serving customers?

Looking Forward

- The economy is still slow. How can you contribute to cost-cutting efforts in the next year?
- Would you benefit by improving your skills in budgeting and financial planning during the next year?
- Your department leads the company in terms of cutting costs without impacting service. What do you need to do this year to keep that up?
- Are you willing to share some of your cost-cutting successes with managers from other departments during the next year?

Creativity

Outstanding

- Is one of our most creative designers
- Exceedingly creative
- Incorporates new data into creative solutions
- Solved a long-standing software glitch through a creative workaround
- Developed promotional concepts that won five clients
- Contributed workplace improvement ideas that saved the department $____
- Improved corporate name recognition by ___ percent in ___ weeks
- Improved manufacturing process to cut downtime by ___ percent
- His ideas spark others to be more creative

Exceeds Expectations

- Sees things from a unique angle
- Accepts criticisms and suggestions about her ideas
- Has come up with imaginative ideas for difficult problems
- Has come up with unique solutions for recurring issues
- Has solved many problems by looking from unique perspective
- Often supplies the creative edge our clients want
- Redesigned work flow between departments that cut approval time 10 percent
- Her creative solutions address both appearance and function
- Adept at teasing out ideas from others

Meets Expectations

- Creative contributions consistent with job requirements
- Imaginative vision
- Developed a number of new ideas for old problems
- Adds a creative flair to projects

- Always experimenting with new approaches
- Generated a pleasing template for customer letters
- Has a good eye for color
- Has developed a number of creative solutions
- Generated a number of creative solutions for clients

Needs Improvement

- Prefers what he knows over new, potentially better ideas
- Lacks creativity
- Rarely has new ideas
- Could strengthen ability to see what's not obvious
- Needs to be more open to others' ideas
- Tends to be staid, does not think outside the box
- Ideas seldom help improve a project
- Mostly modifies others' ideas, rarely generates them
- Clients rarely accept his ideas
- Sometimes a creative liability due to his criticism of others' ideas

Unacceptable

- Creativity far below what job requires
- Unimaginative
- Formats tend to be unstylish and dull
- Sees only what's there, not what is possible
- Does not suggest creative solutions to problems
- Fearful of the new and different
- Has not solved any old problems
- Locked into tried and true, not new
- Never contributes a creative idea
- Clients have not accepted her ideas
- Dampens creativity in others through constant criticism

Self-Monitoring/Self-Evaluation

- How have you helped your coworkers come up with more creative solutions in the past year?

- What has been the most important creative solution contributed last year?
- Which creative campaigns do you feel didn't go well during the last year?
- What makes you get stumped or stuck when coming up with creative solutions? When does this happen?

Looking Forward

- How can you help the creative team generate more and better ideas this year?
- What system can you use to make sure that you don't lose or forget your best ideas?
- How can you "recharge" your creative battery so you continue to come up with great ideas?
- When people criticize your ideas in our brainstorming sessions, what can you do to be less defensive?
- Do you feel that we provide you with the proper tools to enhance your creativity? What could we do better?

Customer Relations

Outstanding

- Relates to customers exceedingly well
- Has developed an incredibly loyal customer base
- Always makes customers feel special
- Resourceful in finding solutions to problems
- Always delivers on promises
- Customers often ask for him by name
- Has not had a single customer complaint registered against her in last 12 months
- Excels at and helps other employees deal with frustrating customers

Exceeds Expectations

- Has won us customer loyalty many times
- Graceful and tactful under pressure from customers
- Customer relations a strength
- Always patient, competent, and professional with customers
- Solves customer problems with speed and accuracy
- Represents our company very well
- Received several commendations from customers this year

Meets Expectations

- Usually competent and professional with customers
- An able representative of the company
- Courteous and knowledgeable
- Professional presentation
- Manages all but the most challenging customer situations
- Handles customer relations responsibilities well

Needs Improvement

- Gets annoyed by customers with a lot of questions
- Shows annoyance and impatience with older customers
- Sometimes gets sarcastic
- Presents a sloppy and uncaring image

- Customer relations skills need improvement
- On several occasions has lost temper with customers
- Conducts personal phone conversations while customers wait
- Lacks some product knowledge needed to help customers

Unacceptable

- Frequently impolite
- Very weak customer relations skills
- Condescends to customers
- Ignores customers
- Chews gum while speaking with customers
- Body language inappropriate when dealing with customers
- Voice tone often aggressive or flat when talking to customers

Self-Monitoring/Self-Evaluation

- When you deal with difficult clients, do you feel they can sense your frustration climbing? How can you improve that situation?
- How do you feel about the way you interact with customers? Are you usually calm and in control?
- Are there instances when you've lost your cool with a customer in the last year? What could you do to fix that situation?
- How do you manage your frustrations so you don't take out your anger on the customers?
- Would you say the majority of customers appreciate your style when dealing with problems? How do you know that?

Looking Forward

- How can you continue to upgrade your product knowledge so you can provide better information to our customers?
- We want every one of our customer relations people to be perceived as helpful all the time. What can you do to become more consistent?
- Are you comfortable with us working together so I can coach you on serving customers more effectively?
- I want to spend a day with each salesperson to help develop his or her customer-service skills. Let's schedule a date.

Data Entry

Outstanding

- Extremely fast and accurate
- In top 5 percent for data entry
- Always willing to take on complicated projects
- Enters data for long periods while maintaining excellent accuracy
- Able to solve problems when data comes in with faulty formats

Exceeds Expectations

- Is fast and accurate
- Always enters in proper fields
- Enters correct data in correct fields
- Has good stamina in working through a large amount of data
- Can enter _____ characters in _____ minutes

Meets Expectations

- Correctly enters data
- Takes and enters data correctly from customers
- Maintains good accuracy and speed
- Proofs while entering
- Completes data entry within expected time limits

Needs Improvement

- Is slower than most, with lower-than-average accuracy
- Slow at keying data
- Can't touch-type numbers
- Regularly makes data entry errors
- Too often enters data in incorrect fields

Unacceptable

- Data entries contain an unacceptable number of errors
- Frequently makes mistakes in data entry

- Doesn't catch entry errors
- Doesn't put data in proper fields
- Takes two hours where the standard entry time is 30 minutes

Self-Monitoring/Self-Evaluation

- Your error rates when entering information into databases is a bit higher than your colleagues. Why is this?
- Your error rates and speed are quite a bit lower than your peers. What can you do to improve your error rate and speed?
- Do you find yourself slowed down by interruptions or noise?

Looking Forward

- We need to put together an action plan to get your accuracy and speed up to standard. Have you got any ideas?
- What would help you continue to improve your accuracy?
- I'd like you to think about how you can monitor your progress on a weekly basis so we know how you are doing.

Deadlines: Ability to Meet

Outstanding
- Consistently ahead of schedule
- Volunteers to work with tight deadlines
- Quickly gets and stays on task
- Completed tasks on time when nobody else could

Exceeds Expectations
- Able to block out distractions
- Amazing task focus when needed
- Seems to thrive on pressure deadlines
- Maintains quality with tight time lines

Meets Expectations
- Generally delivers on time
- Meets deadlines well in periods of calm
- Requires little supervision in tough deadline situations
- Informs when delays anticipated

Needs Improvement
- Missed deadlines more than once this year
- Lack of organization skills sometimes causes delays
- Needs to be more independent to meet deadlines
- Hesitant to take on tough deadlines
- Flustered when deadlines are changed
- Does not like pressure of tight deadlines and avoids these tasks

Unacceptable
- Often misses standard deadlines
- Cannot handle any short-deadline tasks or assignments
- Job may be too pressure-packed
- Not suited to any short-deadline work
- Doesn't admit to being behind schedule

Self-Monitoring/Self-Evaluation

- Is there any single factor that affects your ability to meet deadlines?
- To what do you attribute your ability to meet tough deadlines under pressure?
- Is it possible that you can be too single-minded in meeting deadlines and thus other work gets overlooked?
- Identifying causes of delays is an important part of your job. How can you become better at anticipating problems and overcoming them so you meet deadlines?

Looking Forward

- This year I'd like you to come up with a way to measure the monetary cost of missing deadlines. Any ideas?
- Is there some way I can help you maintain your productivity under tight deadlines?
- I'd like you to share your system of organization with others so they can learn how you are so good with deadlines. How could we do that?
- Let's plan on reducing missed deadlines on important projects to zero or close to it. I want you to draw up a tentative plan.

Decision-Making

Outstanding
- Clearly understands the implications of situations and uses sound judgment when deciding what to do
- Makes tough decisions while others pass the buck
- Decisions always appropriate
- Weighs options carefully and thoroughly
- Can decide in the most challenging situations
- Will make decisions about major issues
- Can always be counted on to make good decisions when faced with a dilemma
- Decisions take into account the needs of all stakeholders

Exceeds Expectations
- Will make decision when others are afraid to commit to a course of action
- Analytic and decisive
- Decisions are well thought out
- Considers "human cost" in decisions
- Decisions always result of detailed analysis
- Makes decisions quickly and appropriately
- Involves others in decision-making

Meets Expectations
- Usually makes appropriate decisions
- Gathers ample information to make reasoned decisions
- Considers many alternatives
- Involves others appropriately when making decisions
- Bases decisions on facts not personalities
- Communicates decisions clearly and directly

Needs Improvement
- Delays making necessary decisions
- Often comes to management for help with a decision

- Sticks with status quo rather than make a decision
- Uses gut rather than facts for decision-making
- Always accepts others' decisions
- Tends to deny responsibility when her decisions don't work out

Unacceptable

- Always worried about making a mistake
- Does not make logical decisions
- Often fails to see problems that require decisions
- Fails to gather necessary information for decision-making
- Frequently makes bad decisions
- Never makes a decision
- Avoids decision-making situations

Self-Monitoring/Self-Evaluation

- Do you feel you have become better at making important job decisions in the last year? How did you accomplish that?
- Is there one decision you had to make during the last year that stands out as the biggest challenge?
- If you could take back any decision you made last year, what would it be? Why?
- Are there times when you feel overwhelmed with making certain kinds of decisions? When does that happen?

Looking Forward

- I'd like to work with you during the year so you can see how I go about analyzing situations to make tough decisions.
- You might want to pick Mary's brain about how she goes about making decisions about her clients, since she's really good at it.
- We need you to continue to develop and make more decisions on your own. Do you have any thoughts on how we could do that?

Dedication to Job/Work

Outstanding

- Is a go-getter in the best sense of the term
- Completes extensive research on potential clients before making a sales call
- Manages to focus on multiple projects without losing track
- Works overtime whenever asked
- Extremely dedicated and committed
- Follows directions precisely
- Questions unclear instructions
- Three days out of five, works until 8:00 P.M. to complete tasks
- Spurs others on to work harder

Exceeds Expectations

- Assumes personal responsibility
- Very committed
- Does whatever is necessary to satisfy customers
- Always shows a can-do attitude
- Routinely works late
- Learns about new technologies affecting work
- Often skips breaks in order to minimize backlogs
- Came in on two Saturdays for extra practice
- Studies user manuals to gain greater skills in our database program

Meets Expectations

- Keeps promises
- Dedicated to goals
- Obeys policies
- Requested training to advance computer skills
- Shows pride in work
- Works regularly scheduled hours
- Completes work well enough to pass minimum standards

Needs Improvement

- Sometimes forgets the overall team/department goals
- Lacks commitment to tasks she doesn't like to do
- Rarely shows genuine enthusiasm for work tasks
- Does the minimum required
- Leaves rework for next shift rather than stay longer
- On occasion forgets to follow directions
- Frequently engages in personal phone calls
- Needs to be reminded to return to work promptly at breaks

Unacceptable

- Doesn't keep current on projects
- Apathetic about performance improvement
- His work is very slow and inaccurate
- Works only when given a warning
- Leaves work for client undone at end of day
- Missed ___ out of ___ team meetings

Self-Monitoring/Self-Evaluation

- I know you have had some family health issues. Do you feel that we've been as supportive as possible?
- Which of your responsibilities do you find a little tedious?
- What can you do to keep work in perspective and recharge your batteries?
- Do you feel that your excitement about the job has dropped during the last year? How can we improve the situation?

Looking Forward

- I've noticed you seem to be less interested in your work these days. What can we do together to get you back to how you were functioning a few years ago?
- Can we enrich your job somehow so you can enjoy it and have new challenges?
- We really need you to show the commitment you showed to your job this past year. How can I help you fight potential burnout next year?

Delegation

Outstanding

- Direct reports gained considerable skill through delegated responsibilities
- Delegates appropriate and challenging responsibilities
- Has strengthened department considerably through effective delegation
- Gives employees energizing and challenging assignments
- Always follows up on results of delegated projects
- Has divided the department's work among five task forces

Exceeds Expectations

- Frequently passes assignments from upper management to able staff members
- Uses delegation to develop staff
- Allows staff to take authority to fulfill responsibilities
- Keeps staff energized with new projects
- Rarely delegates menial tasks
- Creates challenging projects to delegate
- Takes into account employee skills before delegating

Meets Expectations

- Usually keeps workload manageable by enlisting help
- Delegates responsibility with required authority
- Considers staff's capabilities before delegating
- Mixes the mundane and challenging
- Delegates fairly

Needs Improvement

- Fails to check on progress of delegated assignments
- Needs to delegate more challenging assignments
- Fails to give clear directions or goals when delegating
- Stockpiles projects, waiting for time to complete them
- Makes many needless changes in others' work

Unacceptable

- Never delegates and is far behind schedule
- Doesn't consider employees' capabilities when assigning work
- Delegates without direction or support
- Saves all complex, challenging projects for himself
- Has failed to meet goals because of lack of delegation

Self-Monitoring/Self-Evaluation

- Tell me about your biggest success with delegation this last year? Why was that delegation successful?
- Can you recall a situation where you delegated but didn't do a good job preparing the staff member? What happened?
- Do you find yourself delegating tasks that you hate doing, or tasks that someone else can do just as well as you?
- The workload is very high, and I notice you avoid delegating tasks to your staff and end up working long hours. Why is that?

Looking Forward

- I'd like to see you delegate more important tasks to your subordinates so you can focus on the things only you can do. How do you think you can accomplish this?
- How can you prepare your staff to take on more delegated responsibility?
- Will you be able to continue to delegate to your senior staff during the upcoming year, since it seems to be going very well?

Dependability

Outstanding

- Willingly takes accountability for all departmental activities
- Can always be counted on to complete assignments
- Always delivers on promises
- Achieves results with minimal resources
- Always achieves stated goals and more
- Assumes personal responsibility for his/her work
- Performs work independently and accurately
- Takes action and makes decisions quickly
- Always delivers on time
- Followed up personally with more than ___ customers

Exceeds Expectations

- Delivers on promises far more often than not
- High level of accountability for projects
- Does not disappoint when deadlines are tight
- Almost always adheres to instructions/directions
- Performs most work independently
- Delivered ___ of ___ completed reports on time
- Missed only ___ days of work in last year

Meets Expectations

- Appropriate level of accountability
- Delivers on promises
- Adheres to policies and guidelines
- Conscientious worker
- Accountable for projects
- Follows directions and instructions
- Needs little oversight on projects

Needs Improvement

- Fails to accept accountability for missed deadlines
- Does not accept accountability for project failures
- Frequently fails to achieve goals

- Does not follow directions or instructions
- Needs oversight
- Doesn't take action or make decisions without direction
- Has missed deadlines ___ times
- Returned late from breaks ___ times in the year

Unacceptable
- Fails to accept accountability for own behavior or results
- Always attributes failure to others or circumstances
- Rarely delivers a project on time
- Does not achieve agreed-upon goals
- Frequently does not follow directions or instructions
- Needs constant oversight
- Rarely takes action or makes decisions without direction
- Needs frequent reminders to keep projects on track
- Uses the phone for personal conversations

Self-Monitoring/Self-Evaluation
- If dependability means being consistent and trusted by coworkers, how do you think you've done this last year?
- When you have missed deadlines, what in particular has contributed to the missed deadlines?
- You have the skills to be the trusted go-to guy when things get tough. Do you think you have reached a level of dependability for others to see you that way? Why?

Looking Forward
- During the next year I'd like to see you have fewer things fall through the cracks so we can rely on you when the going gets rough. How can we accomplish that?
- What can you do during the next year to cut down on missed deadlines?
- It's important for you to communicate when things will be delayed or other problems. I need a commitment from you to keep me better informed in those situations. How can you do that?

Development of Subordinates

Outstanding

- Exceedingly devoted to staff development
- Creative and dedicated to developing others
- Training and delegation combine to develop an excellent staff
- Always registers new employees for appropriate training
- Inspires staff to learn
- Always shares relevant company information with subordinates
- Finds low-cost ways to develop staff

Exceeds Expectations

- Invests time during all appraisals on personal development
- Has an "open door" to new employees who have questions about the job
- Reinforces and supports new-employee orientation
- Uses delegation well to develop staff
- Excellent role model for continuous learning

Meets Expectations

- Gives employees advanced training and additional responsibilities
- Develops employees appropriately
- Regularly shares management information during staff meetings
- Every employee in the department received training in Excel

Needs Improvement

- Insufficient training has led to poor productivity
- Fails to develop staff in needed areas
- Does not appropriately develop staff to perform needed duties

- Her department suffered a 10 percent error rate due to inadequate training
- Does not provide adequate feedback to help learning

Unacceptable
- Staff is poorly trained
- Delegates only menial tasks
- Error rate in department is unacceptable
- Received numerous customer complaints about staff's capability and courtesy
- Has repeatedly delayed giving new employees orientation to the department

Self-Monitoring/Self-Evaluation
- On average how much time do you spend helping staff learn the things they need to excel at their jobs?
- In what ways do you see a positive impact from your attending to and helping people learn new skills?
- What nontraditional learning methods have you used to develop your staff during the last year?

Looking Forward
- We don't have a budget for training this year. How can you continue to support your staff in learning new skills they need for their jobs?
- Part of your job is to ensure there are staff who can step in and substitute for you for certain management tasks. How can you prepare people to do that?
- When staff participate in training this year, how can you ensure that what they learn (and the investment) doesn't go to waste?

Equal Opportunity/Diversity

Outstanding
- An excellent model of EEO practices
- Invites diverse ideas
- Ensures staff represents percentage of protected classes in population
- Sensitive to and respectful of all individuals
- Formed a task force to attract minority achievers

Exceeds Expectations
- Provides equal opportunities to members of protected classes
- Is free of bias in personnel evaluations
- Maintains pay equity for all staff in similar positions
- Ensures that staff from disadvantaged backgrounds receive appropriate training

Meets Expectations
- Bases all personnel decisions on performance
- Supports EEO and diversity values
- Shows no indication of bias
- Makes decisions based on performance, not personal characteristics
- Has hired from diverse ethnic backgrounds

Needs Improvement
- Needs to strengthen EEO/diversity orientation
- Has only white males in supervisory positions
- Members of protected classes and women are paid less
- Minorities enrolled in fewer training sessions
- Department lacks ethnic diversity

Unacceptable
- Has blatantly discriminated
- Will not interview minority candidates

- Has told off-color jokes in staff meetings
- Minorities consistently receive lower performance ratings
- Several lawsuits cite his failure to promote Hispanic workers despite their merit

Self-Monitoring/Self-Evaluation

- Your department has the lowest percentage of women in management positions in the company. Why is that?
- What could you have done to address Mary Smith's legal suit before it was filed?
- What is your opinion of the hiring guidelines we put in place last year for hiring and recruiting more minorities?
- What barriers have you faced in HR that have impacted your ability to hire people from other cultures?
- Do you feel our equal opportunity policies make it harder for you to do your job? Why?

Looking Forward

- What can you do this year to help us reach our goal of having employees from various backgrounds in our company?
- Recruitment can be a problem for hiring minorities. What are your ideas about how we can recruit people with varying backgrounds?
- The equal opportunity laws change a lot so it's important to keep current. I'd like you to attend an equal opportunity seminar at least once every two years, so I'd like you to identify resources for you and other managers.

Ethical Behavior

Outstanding

- Exceptionally scrupulous and honest in all activities
- Does what's right regardless of consequences
- Always demonstrates integrity and honesty
- Is exceptionally conscientious in potential conflict of interest situations
- Has received high praise for swift and generous remedies for product defects
- Has retained or gained new customers due to honesty
- Excellent role model for her staff on ethical issues
- Challenges coworkers to meet stringent ethical standards

Exceeds Expectations

- Never lies or bends the truth
- Argues vigorously for fair dealing
- Created a clear values statement for staff about ethics
- Knows and follows applicable laws
- Customers have been happily surprised by honesty
- Employees see her as standing for doing the right thing even if it is difficult

Meets Expectations

- Deals with customers fairly
- Will not exploit loopholes in laws for benefit
- Staff understands and follows ethical guidelines
- Is noted for honesty and fairness
- Employees respect her position on fair and honest advertising

Needs Improvement

- Sometimes sees ethics as an inconvenience
- Has been known to stretch the law for gain
- Has behaved unethically in dealings with clients
- Complaints have been lodged about this store's bait-and-switch tactics

- Has encouraged staff to cut ethical corners for profit's sake
- Sometimes comes off to staff a bit holier-than-thou on ethical issues

Unacceptable
- Does not behave ethically
- Has lied to others in department
- Violates the company's code of ethics
- The state's attorney general has initiated legal action
- Actions have resulted in customers refusing to do business with us
- Consistently makes poor ethical decisions
- Auditors have identified suspicious practices in departmental accounting under her control
- Talks a good game about ethics and then crosses too many ethical lines

Self-Monitoring/Self-Evaluation
- Just to check, have you declared any potential conflict of interest situations you might be involved in for last year?
- When you face tough ethical choices, do you tend to consult with others to see how they might handle the situations? Give an example.
- Have there been any ethics-related situations where we have lost customers due to being too stringent or too lax?

Looking Forward
- Do you have any thoughts on how we can update our ethics policies by the end of the year?
- Do we have too many controls to prevent unethical behavior, is it just right, or are we too lax?
- What can you do this coming year to encourage ethical behavior in your staff?
- Have you read the ethics guidelines, and how are you prepared to apply them in terms of your own behavior and that of your staff?

Feedback: Giving and Receiving

Outstanding

- Always offers criticism in a constructive manner
- Consistently receives feedback constructively
- Involves staff in deciding how to improve work output and quality
- Initiates changes based on all feedback
- Welcomes feedback, especially negative
- Often asks for feedback, listens, and implements when possible

Exceeds Expectations

- Delivers feedback in a sensitive and caring way
- Translates criticism into positive changes
- Seeks to understand rather than defend against negative feedback
- Uses feedback to reinforce behavioral changes
- Accepts all negative feedback positively
- Listens to feedback but does not implement change without thought
- Infrequently offers feedback but when she does, coworkers listen carefully

Meets Expectations

- Usually is receptive to and appreciative of feedback
- Provides feedback to subordinates as necessary
- Works to learn from feedback received
- Delivers negative comments to staff while maintaining positive relations
- Can turn most criticism into appropriate action
- Does not emotionally overload employees

Needs Improvement

- Is often silent when constructive criticism is called for
- Will criticize the person and not his or her actions
- Delivers negative feedback in a personally hurtful manner

- Tends to deliver feedback in an insensitive way
- Disagrees with constructive criticism, rather than accepting
- On occasion has ignored feedback and caused negative business results

Unacceptable

- Never offers criticism in a constructive manner
- Consistently receives feedback defensively and argumentatively
- Consistently avoids providing necessary feedback
- Does not speak with staff about how to improve work output and quality
- Consistently takes feedback with negativity and disagreement
- Uses patronizing tone when giving feedback
- Dislike of feedback has resulted in an inability to improve her performance

Self-Monitoring/Self-Evaluation

- What are your strongest points related to giving feedback to your staff? What are the weakest?
- How would you evaluate yourself on your ability to listen to feedback and improve your performance based on that?
- How do you check for understanding when you give or receive feedback?

Looking Forward

- I expect that you will communicate your expectations and give ongoing feedback to your employees. How can you accomplish that?
- Giving feedback to staff is one of the top job responsibilities for supervisors here. I want you to develop a plan to increase the time and positive effects of feedback in your department.
- How do you plan to increase your receptivity to feedback from your staff?
- Are you getting enough feedback on a regular basis from me? What can I do to make it better?

Financial Management

Outstanding
- Anticipates financial problems before they occur
- Provides meaningful information to decision-makers
- Involves staff in financial improvement initiatives
- Implements prudent risk analysis
- Despite unexpected technical problems still managed to get critical financial reports in on time

Exceeds Expectations
- Gets the most from scarce resources
- Implemented measures for financial accountability
- Uses accounting information to make decisions
- Actual expenditures within 10 percent of budget projections
- Notifies project managers of cost overruns in a timely fashion
- Willingness to spend money to increase the bottom line

Meets Expectations
- Understands and uses standard accounting practices
- Prepares budget projections on time
- Translates raw financial data into information for others
- Follows standard financial practices
- Stays current on financial issues during year
- Prepares appropriate year-end statements
- Accurately reports financial status of department

Needs Improvement
- Exceeded budget by 20 percent last year
- Loses sight of financial big picture
- Focuses on financial health of his own work unit at the expense of other work units
- Could control expenditures better
- Has difficulty understanding "the books"
- His financial reports tend to gloss over bad news

Unacceptable

- Often runs in deficit mode
- Uncooperative with company auditors
- Does not inform superiors of potential problems
- Has ignored serious accounting errors
- Financial reports are intentionally misleading
- Does not accept responsibility for financial problems

Self-Monitoring/Self-Evaluation

- In the last year, what has caused your financial reports to be late?
- How can you be more on top of what your staff are doing so we get timely and accurate financials?
- How well do you think we managed the transition from the old financial software to the new? How could we have done better?

Looking Forward

- How do you plan to implement the auditor's suggestions on financial management in your division?
- The monthly financial reports are critical, and we need them at month's end every month. What do you need to change to meet these requirements?
- Tax and financial markets are in flux these days. What do you need to keep on top of things as they happen?

Flexibility

Outstanding
- When asked to work unusual hours, always complies
- Is among the most flexible members of our team
- Drops current work to promptly address emergencies
- Shifted from the 8–4 shift to the midnight–8 shift when requested without complaint

Exceeds Expectations
- Has mastered different approaches to situations and can flexibly respond as required
- Able to shift focus rapidly
- Willingly assumes others' tasks in case of absences
- Accommodates shifting priorities when other staff members are unavailable

Meets Expectations
- Gracefully accepts changes to work
- Will reset priorities as required
- Adjusts to changes in procedure fairly well
- Often changes schedule to meet production deadlines

Needs Improvement
- Resists changes
- Argues against resetting priorities
- Becomes agitated when asked to work outside the daily routine
- Frequently will not change mind, despite new evidence

Unacceptable
- Lacks flexibility in most situations
- Won't change priorities until disciplined
- Failure to shift priorities has lost us two clients
- Refused to follow new procedure

Self-Monitoring/Self-Evaluation

- How would you evaluate yourself in terms of being flexible with the often-changing priorities of the job?
- Can you give me an example of how you moved out of your comfort zone to do something different when the situation required it?
- Do you feel you have enough tools in your toolbox to change strategies in the middle of a project if it's called for? Give me an example of when you did that.

Looking Forward

- How do you look for alternative ways to solve a problem when your original strategy seems to be going nowhere?
- I'd like you to be more flexible in terms of evaluating the ideas of others, particularly the ones that seem foreign to you.
- More in-depth analysis might help you come up with other ways to meet goals that are different and more effective than what you usually do. How can we get there?

Goal and Objective Setting

Outstanding
- Basically self-directing
- Goals he sets are always relevant to the organization's big picture
- Seems to automatically know what must be achieved
- Always seems clear about what to do
- Often asks questions that help the group clarify goals

Exceeds Expectations
- Coaches others in setting sensible goals
- Good at putting objectives into words
- Communicates objectives and goals effectively
- Understands link between goals and planning tasks
- Skilled at mapping out goals and plans of action

Meets Expectations
- Accepts goals set out by supervisor
- Goals chosen are realistic
- Achieves most goals assigned
- Alters goal priorities as needed
- Is guided by goals and objectives

Needs Improvement
- Could show more initiative in setting own goals
- Often asks others what to do next
- Hesitant to work with manager to set goals
- Sets vague or unmeasurable objectives
- Goals and objectives need to be examined by supervisor

Unacceptable
- Sets goals that are impossible to achieve
- Unaware of organization's goals and objectives
- Has no interest in setting goals
- Pays no attention to company or unit objectives

- Doesn't make the link between goals and job success
- Just wants to do his/her own thing
- Sets goals below her capabilities

Self-Monitoring/Self-Evaluation

- How can you make sure that the work you do contributes to the overall goals of the work unit?
- Are there times you have felt unsure as to why you were doing a certain task and why it was important?
- How well have I done in communicating what's important and what's not in terms of your objectives?

Looking Forward

- What can I do to make it clearer how your job tasks and goals fit into the overall strategy of the company?
- When you find yourself unsure of what your job priorities are and which goals to focus on, we need a way for you to clarify them ahead of time. How can we do that?
- I know you are a bit of a maverick and like to do your own thing and that can be valuable. We need you to be working toward overall company goals without sacrificing your creativity and autonomy. Do you have any ideas about how we can do that?

Grooming and Appearance

Outstanding
- Impeccable dress and grooming
- Exhibits good taste and appropriateness in attire
- Immediately conveys positive impression
- Fashionable, yet understated appearance
- Projects a very positive image for company

Exceeds Expectations
- A polished appearance
- Appears composed and professional
- Appears, and is, knowledgeable and confident
- Dresses properly for all business occasions
- Matches attire to situation and business expectations

Meets Expectations
- Comes to work properly attired
- Meets all our guidelines for grooming and appearance
- Carries him/herself with confidence
- Clothes are clean and pressed
- Presents a professional image

Needs Improvement
- Grooming and appearance need to be improved
- Idiosyncratic sense of style puts off some customers
- Often has a sloppy appearance
- Pants and shirt are often mismatched
- Others have asked to be seated far away from him/her
- Number of piercings and tattoos have solicited negative comments from customers
- Has a tendency to overdress for casual meetings on worksites
- Sometimes alienates others by overdressing in the field
- Older clients feel she dresses provocatively and have commented

Unacceptable

- Ignored requests to deal with appearance
- Will often underdress for important meetings
- Disheveled and unclean appearance
- Presents a poor image of our company
- Clothes are often dirty and wrinkled
- Some have reported unpleasant body odor
- Appearance and clothing upset or frighten customers and coworkers
- Wears T-shirts with unacceptable slogans despite requests to stop

Self-Monitoring/Self-Evaluation

- Tell me about an occasion where you felt your appearance either helped or hindered working with customers?
- We've had some complaints from customers about your choice of apparel, particularly the rude slogans on your T-shirts. Do you feel that's an issue for you?
- I feel that you tend to overdress for the nature of your job. Please read the section in the employee handbook dealing with job-appropriate attire.

Looking Forward

- I'd like to encourage you to choose what you wear based on your job tasks. What things can you take into account?
- In future, if you dress casually for the office, you might want to keep a suit in the office. Then you can change into it when you have an unexpected client meeting.
- Your taste in clothes is really good, but let's not forget that your clothing can hamper you from doing your job. What are some situations where you can dress more conservatively and appropriately?

Initiative

Outstanding

- Always seeking ways to show initiative
- Negotiated a ___ percent discount with vendors, saving us $___ per year
- Knows when and how to take action
- Shows strong initiative in every situation
- Have not ever needed to request that he acts proactively
- Worked an extra ___ hours to eliminate error messages in database
- Developed a new work process for communications between accounting and marketing
- Foresaw crisis with client X and express-shipped part to ensure there was no work stoppage—client praised her
- Called together representatives from three departments and solved problem with client X

Exceeds Expectations

- Takes initiative frequently and appropriately
- Often displays foresight in heading off problems before they occur
- Is above the norm in showing initiative
- Does not shy away from taking risks
- Without instruction, negotiated lower rates with ___ of ___ vendors
- Redesigned existing software to solve serious customer problem

Meets Expectations

- Takes initiative when appropriate
- Comfortable making decisions to solve customers' problems
- Will take appropriate action without seeking permission first
- Likes limits specifically spelled out, but goes to them willingly

- The times she's taken initiative to improve things, it has always turned out well
- Will take risks to accommodate customers
- Created a project oversight committee and its mission statement with minimal direction
- Instituted extranet connection for vendor X to improve project coordination
- Can take initiative when called for

Needs Improvement
- Does only what's asked
- Rarely takes any action unless specifically told to
- Needs to take initiative more often
- Slow to act
- Rarely shows initiative
- Doesn't make decisions without approval
- Should take action more often to resolve problems without first getting permission
- Failed to solve customer X's problem
- Not yet confident enough to make decisions
- Shows initiative at a level below what the job requires

Unacceptable
- Shows initiative at a level far below what the job requires
- Does not take initiative to resolve issues
- Needs to be told everything step-by-step in precise detail
- Displays no initiative
- No independent action
- Often will see him waiting for work, rather than figuring out what needs to be done
- Waits until directed to act
- Delays decisions until it's too late
- Lost a large customer because of lack of initiative
- Takes no initiative to solve customers' problems

Self-Monitoring/Self-Evaluation

- What were some of the moments you recall last year when you showed initiative? How about when you wish you'd taken more of it?

- How do you see the level of initiative you've taken compared to your colleagues?

- How clearly do you think we describe the amount of initiative we expect from you here?

- Can you think of some times last year when you weren't sure what your authority was to make decisions? Can we talk about some of them?

- I know you feel hampered by the limits on authority we have here. Let's talk about why these are in place so you feel less uncomfortable with these limits.

Looking Forward

- How can I help you identify and zone in on the level of authority you have? I'm concerned that you're not using all that you have.

- What would you like to be able to do in the upcoming year in terms of taking direct responsibility for resolving customer complaints?

- I'd like to see you take more responsibility for getting your projects completed on time. What would help you get there? How can I help?

Interpersonal Skills

Outstanding
- Often requested as a work partner
- Gets along very well with everyone—associates, customers, and vendors
- Excellent conflict management skills
- Managers consistently find him helpful, friendly, and reasonable
- Effective interaction with people no matter the status
- Consistently effective in finding the right things to say to motivate others to do exceptional work
- Relates well to everyone regardless of his or her background
- Is absolutely blind to others' differences
- Genuinely interested in what others have to say
- Often receive unsolicited positive feedback about her from others

Exceeds Expectations
- Works well with others in all aspects of job
- Seeks first to understand
- Corrects others tactfully and professionally
- Three times this year, have heard good things about how positive it is working with him
- Assertive, but sensitive to others
- Open to Improving Interpersonal skills
- Accepts people from other backgrounds
- Is accepted by people from other cultures

Meets Expectations
- Does not make sexist or racist comments
- Has a good sense of humor that's always appropriate
- Gets along OK in most situations
- Communicates well with others
- A little awkward in some difficult interpersonal situations

Needs Improvement

- Doesn't always listen carefully
- Quick to lose patience with others
- Twice this year we've had to speak to her about weak interactions with others
- Sometimes tells inappropriate jokes
- Doesn't use skills in emotionally charged situations
- Body language and words don't always match
- Some believe tone is arrogant

Unacceptable

- Often makes insensitive criticisms of others
- Talks behind people's backs
- Every month people have reported inappropriate comments or behaviors from him
- Received justified complaints from coworkers
- Has not paid attention to coaching
- Consistently passive-aggressive
- Tries to look good by attacking others

Self-Monitoring/Self-Evaluation

- How do you think others view your interpersonal skills?
- Can you think of a couple of times last year when your communication skills were either particularly strong or weak?
- Who among your coworkers this year do you think you've created a strong relationship with and why do you think that happened?
- A number of customers have mentioned some comments you've made that they thought were inappropriate. What prompted you to make such comments?

Looking Forward

- How can I help you improve your interpersonal skills with others?

- You do a good job communicating with customers. I'd like you to develop and deliver a mini-seminar on the techniques you use.
- Please list some things you're willing to do to better connect with our customers.
- I'd like to hear from a customer this month about how helpful and professional you were. How might you go about meeting that challenge?

Judgment

Outstanding

- Shows strong judgment in the most difficult situations
- Excels at balancing risk and reward
- Always does a thorough, thoughtful analysis of complicated situations
- Helped company avert a costly strike through skillful negotiation
- Consistently has a clear understanding of the implications of decisions

Exceeds Expectations

- Demonstrates mature, seasoned judgment
- Five times last year she demonstrated exceptional judgment in resolving problems with five customers
- Made good decisions in a number of difficult cases
- Judges situations clearly and proceeds accordingly
- Interceded effectively in a number of "political" clashes
- Makes decisions based on facts and the interests of our company and customers

Meets Expectations

- Examines all sides of a situation before making a decision
- Shows clear judgment in resolving conflict
- Sees most situations clearly enough to resolve issues satisfactorily
- Appropriately elevated customers' concerns to executive-level contact
- Strengthened our relationship with accounting by authorizing overtime to complete project X on time

Needs Improvement

- Sometimes shows poor judgment in dealing with his/her staff

- Showed weak judgment in three significant cases with customers last year
- Needs to "consider the source" more often when judging situations
- Has made some snap judgments that have created customer dissatisfaction
- Finds it difficult to be nonjudgmental when judgment dictates neutrality
- Needs to strengthen situational awareness

Unacceptable

- Has lacked sound judgment on a number of critical occasions
- Will often fail to fully investigate before initiating action
- Doesn't verify information before making decisions
- On four notable occasions, misjudged a customer's complaint and created a bigger problem
- Has shown poor judgment in a number of client interactions
- Got into a shouting match with a VP at a board meeting
- Poor judgment resulted in lowered group performance in a number of cases

Self-Monitoring/Self-Evaluation

- You've made a number of judgment calls to get your job done. What process do you go through before deciding how far to take something to get it resolved?
- What decision-making process do you go through with customers to ensure they're satisfied?
- Tell me what information you were working with when you decided how to resolve the issue with X. What did you decide to do as a result of that information?
- How did your judgment call to push things with customer X work out and why do you think it concluded that way?

Looking Forward

- Based on your decision-making experience last year, what would you like to focus on this year to strengthen those types of decisions?
- How can I help you improve the judgment you exercise to fulfill your job duties?
- What changes would you suggest to improve our customer satisfaction ratings?
- You rarely exercise the authority you have. How can you improve on that this year?

Knowledge of Company Processes

Outstanding

- His knowledge of processes is unsurpassed
- Has clear sense of how his work contributes to the sucess of the company and frequently makes suggestions for improvement
- Has been nominated to three cross-functional teams
- Implemented three major work flow changes that eliminated double work and speeded delivery
- Excellent person to answer questions about company
- Applied knowledge to improve company-wide processes
- Frequently is the first to identify process problems others have missed

Exceeds Expectations

- Has often found ways to improve our processes
- Understands the influences on decision-making very well
- Serves as liaison to marketing, sales, and manufacturing
- Has a good understanding of how our departments interact and uses that knowledge to get things done
- Uses knowledge of big picture to guide action

Meets Expectations

- Sufficiently understands processes to work effectively
- Has suggested a few improvements in our work flow
- Knows interactions between his/her function and others in department
- Understands finance and marketing well, but needs more background on manufacturing
- Changed label location so shipping could find it more easily

Needs Improvement

- Is still learning our work flow
- Will check on how to enter data correctly quite a few times

- Unfamiliar with a few basic processes
- Still learning his/her way around
- Needs to learn more about our clients' expectations of us

Unacceptable

- Is unfamiliar with how his function affects others
- Makes changes without checking with those affected
- Her lack of understanding of other departments' information requirements have resulted in a number of difficult customer situations
- Doesn't understand the link between sales and development
- Repeated two past failures due to lack of research

Self-Monitoring/Self-Evaluation

- What specific steps can you take to learn company processes and how to improve your contribution to these processes?
- How can you increase your understanding of how this affects the performance of your teammates and other team members?
- I want you to commit to making at least one suggestion a month to improve organizational processes.

Looking Forward

- You have a broad knowledge of the workings of this company. Would you be willing to lead a discussion next week at our staff meeting to share some of your company knowledge?
- What can I do to help you learn about how we do things around here?
- I want you to set up meetings with company department heads to learn better how what we do affects them and develop ways we can improve our processes.
- What can you do to improve your knowledge of our company processes?

Knowledge of Job

Outstanding
- Has complete mastery of his/her job
- Has a great wealth of knowledge about all job facets
- Some have forgotten more than others know; he hasn't forgotten anything
- Her level of knowledge is outstanding
- He is an expert in the functioning of system X
- Has authoritative understanding of job responsibilities
- Is a great source of information for others in our department
- Has kept XYZ certification current for 10 years in a row
- Gained certification in XYZ-2.0 this year

Exceeds Expectations
- Understands all aspects of job
- Willingly shares her great knowledge of our department's processes
- Strong level of job knowledge
- Knowledge exceeds what is required to perform well

Meets Expectations
- Level of job knowledge appropriate to perform tasks required
- Understands X and Y very well
- Maintains knowledge through seminars and courses
- Knows most of the systems necessary to succeed
- Keeps up-to-date through reading industry periodicals

Needs Improvement
- Needs to learn more to perform job satisfactorily
- Often runs into situations where he doesn't know what to do
- A number of times last year has shown his knowledge to be out of date

Needs to improve job knowledge

- Only attends seminars begrudgingly
- Infrequently has the job knowledge to know what to do
- Needs to ask for help on many projects
- Makes more errors than average

Unacceptable

- Needs to learn much more to perform job satisfactorily
- Made no effort to keep up-to-date on changes in her field
- Is many years out-of-date with knowledge
- Rarely has the job knowledge to know what to do
- Needs to ask for help far more frequently than acceptable
- Makes many more errors than average

Self-Monitoring/Self-Evaluation

- There have been a few times this year that you didn't have current knowledge to advise customers correctly. What have you been doing to learn more about our products?
- You know a lot about our computer system. How did you gain such a strong understanding of it?
- In what areas of your job do you feel weakest in terms of knowledge? What would help you learn more about them?
- If you had to pick a product you feel you know the most about, what would it be? How about the product you know least about?

Looking Forward

- What areas of job knowledge do you plan to work on strengthening this year?
- How could I help you learn more about your job?
- What am I not doing that you wish I would do to help you better understand our services?
- I'd like you to prepare a short talk for our next staff meeting about X. You know it so well and I know others would benefit from your knowledge.

Leadership Skills

Outstanding

- Uses participative approach whenever called for
- Clearly understands leading as "facilitating the success of team and company"
- Has employees fired up and committed to organizational goals and vision
- Sees herself as a facilitator of employee and company success
- Turns on employee motivation to aim for excellence
- Persevered through many leadership challenges
- Excellent at training, motivating, and guiding staff
- Builds excellent team spirit and direction
- Accepts blame; shares successes
- Employees show great loyalty to him
- Ranked as superior leader by __ of __ subordinates
- Led group to exceed sales targets in __ of __ regions
- Championed migration to ERP system, completed __ months ahead of target

Exceeds Expectations

- Has the confidence of employees and peers
- Has a participative approach
- Organizes teams with insight into talents and capabilities
- Her professional demeanor sets an example for others
- Considers staff's personal and professional welfare
- Assertive and firm, while fair
- Has authority, but leads without dictating
- Dedicates the time and effort necessary to achieve results
- Willing to make tough decisions
- Exhibits traits that generate confidence
- Headed numerous successful projects

Meets Expectations

- Effectively motivates and directs

- Competently leads staff
- Holds and displays company values
- Satisfactorily overcame some challenges to her leadership
- Shows strengths in leading, motivating, coaching
- Puts worker safety above productivity
- Encourages others to share ideas and approaches
- Could become an excellent leader over the next two years
- Is a developing leader; strong in some areas already

Needs Improvement
- Isn't secure about being in front of a group
- Needs to develop a number of leadership characteristics
- Sometimes fails to inform staff of changes
- Will sometimes put productivity ahead of staff welfare and safety
- Rarely assists to resolve disputes among employees
- Needs to ask what others think more often
- Led well, but in the wrong direction
- Sets unrealistic goals
- Rarely involves staff in decision-making

Unacceptable
- Dictates rather than leads
- Appears totally unable to build teams and direct others' activities
- Doesn't command respect
- Fails to train, motivate, or direct staff
- Will not solicit opinions from others
- Fails to see that leading should be preceded by listening and learning
- Has minimized safety concerns to meet production goals
- Sets goals contrary to company mission
- Has failed to lead in several situations where that was necessary
- Never involves others in making decisions

- Is usually late in giving staff vital information
- Three employees of his have complained about the way he leads their team
- Behavior generates frequent employee complaints
- Has lost respect of employees

Self-Monitoring/Self-Evaluation

- What was the major reason your projects all progressed as well as they did this year?
- You had a hard time with some of your staff this year. Why was that?
- A number of your employees have progressed very well this year. How were you involved with that progress?
- If you had it to do over again, what would you have done differently with X?

Looking Forward

- What aspects of your leadership skills would you like to develop this year?
- What were the biggest leadership challenges you've had this year? How might you do things differently based on what you've learned?
- What can I do to help improve your leadership skills?

Listening Skills

Outstanding
- Remarkable listening skills
- Hears, remembers, and understands virtually everything
- Listens and understands even when upset
- Creates a climate where employees listen to each other
- Able to empathize with other's situations
- Is always attentive, even in difficult situations

Exceeds Expectations
- Regarded as a very good listener by everyone
- Accurately interprets what is said
- Makes frequent use of active/reflective listening
- Only needs to be told something once
- Honestly interested in what others say

Meets Expectations
- Understands and can use active/reflective listening
- Hears and follows directions accurately
- Questions when unsure of understanding
- Remembers what others have said

Needs Improvement
- Doesn't use listening skills in "tough" situations
- Sometimes so anxious to speak that he/she stops listening
- Needs things explained several times
- Sometimes distracted and doesn't hear or understand what was said

Unacceptable
- Constantly interrupts
- Often misinterprets what was said due to weak listening skills
- Poor attention span
- Drifts off during important meetings when not speaking
- Not aware when she/he doesn't understand

Self-Monitoring/Self-Evaluation

- You know that I've heard a few negative things about your focus on the phone. Can you tell me what's going on? I'd like to help if I can.
- You seem to listen attentively to and understand our customers. What's your secret?
- I was pleased to overhear that conversation you had with that angry customer last week. You handled it so effectively. What were you thinking while speaking with her?

Looking Forward

- As an organization, what can we do to strengthen the listening skills of those in roles similar to yours?
- A number of times I've needed to repeat or clarify the specifics of what I wanted you to do. Can you tell me how I might communicate better with you?
- You know how important effective listening is to your job. I'd like you to strengthen your ability to its fullest potential. Do you have thoughts on how we might do that?
- Are you willing to speak with your colleagues about the techniques you use to listen so effectively to our customers? There's 15 minutes free at our next group meeting—can I schedule you for that?

Long-Range Planning

Outstanding
- Shows great foresight in planning
- Makes plans far ahead of expected events
- An exceedingly strong strategic planner
- Developed a cost-cutting plan that avoided mandatory lay-offs
- Makes use of long-range plans in everyday decision-making

Exceeds Expectations
- Always looking three to five years down the road
- Thoroughly plans all details far in advance
- Anticipated decline in sector and identified three new markets for our product
- Links long-term planning to shorter-term implementation

Meets Expectations
- Has planned well for contingencies
- Generally has plans ready ahead of the need for them
- A good tactical planner
- Invests sufficient time in long-range planning
- Identified need and developed an Internet browsing workshop

Needs Improvement
- Needs to look further down the road
- Often misses details in long-term plans
- Long-term planning is one of his weak points
- Good with tactics but needs to strengthen strategic plans

Unacceptable
- Has been caught off guard repeatedly by market changes
- Rarely plans for contingencies that are easily anticipated
- Needs to spend time analyzing trends and preparing for them

- Ten-year plan skips the first three years
- Plans long term then ignores it

Self-Monitoring/Self-Evaluation

- You got caught off guard last month. That's unusual for you; what happened?
- It seems you anticipated everything in our recent transition. How did you go about preparing for it?
- What sort of long-range focus do you think our organization has? What sort do you think it needs?
- How do you manage the demands of doing both long-range planning and making sure that all the details are attended to in the short term?

Looking Forward

- There were some things that came up in our meetings last week that you seemed unprepared for. How might you minimize such surprises in the future?
- What can I do to help you plan more effectively for the long term?
- In what areas of long-term planning would you like to see yourself develop in?
- We're bringing together a group of folks from different areas of the organization to plan far ahead and I'd like you to represent us. Are you willing to do that?

Management Control

Outstanding
- Able to track multiple issues and problems
- Identifies potential problems before they occur
- Shares control with employees
- Views control as a means for improving processes
- Expert in the use of statistical process control
- Takes action to prevent problems early in process

Exceeds Expectations
- Manages changing priorities
- Does not overextend himself by overinvolvement
- Chooses staff wisely to take control of responsibilities
- Regularly looks for ways to improve the system

Meets Expectations
- Provides an adequate level of management control
- Unit tends to run smoothly
- Exerts management control as appropriate
- Attends to details when needed

Needs Improvement
- Seeks to control everything, negatively affecting productivity
- Could exercise greater control
- Staff takes advantage of flexibility
- Sometimes relies on the wrong people
- Failed to know that a staff member would be absent from a critical meeting

Unacceptable
- Consistently out of touch with work going on
- Exercises minimal control over staff
- Seen by others as hoarding power
- Unable or unwilling to make fast decisions

- Allows problems to go on too long
- Crises regularly occur in his/her area of responsibility

Self-Monitoring/Self-Evaluation

- How do you think you did with management controls this year?
- Which projects were the most challenging for you to establish controls for this year? Why do you think that was?
- A few times this year, things got out of control in your area. Have you done much thinking about what led up to those issues? What were your conclusions?
- You seem to use just the right amount of control with your folks. How do you go about deciding how much latitude to give?

Looking Forward

- There were a couple of major incidents this year that could have been avoided if we'd known better what was going on ahead of time. What do you suggest we do to get better information and thus better control?
- You seem reluctant to delegate fully to some of your staff and some of them are frustrated by that. Why are you reluctant to delegate tasks and authority?
- To advance with the company, one area I know you'll need to strengthen is using management controls effectively. There's a program coming up in August and I'd like you to participate in it.
- I'd like you to involve your staff more in developing control mechanisms. You're trying to take on all the responsibility yourself and it's gotten to be too much for you to do alone.

Management Skills

Outstanding

- An excellent planner
- Organizes people and resources for efficiency and success
- Stays informed without being intrusive
- Uses time and resources effectively
- Strong at screening and hiring new employees
- Effectively handles employee conflicts
- Helps others take responsibility and action

Exceeds Expectations

- Models desired behavior for staff
- Mastered and uses basic coaching skills
- Skilled in managing resources, people, and workload
- Rarely needs to use formal disciplinary action
- Processes normally operate well with few problems
- Plans well

Meets Expectations

- Always delegates effectively
- Keeps employees in the loop
- Maintains personnel and financial records as required
- Plans normally have few glitches
- Regularly informs superiors of progress/problems
- Usually achieves goals and objectives
- Effective participant in hiring process

Needs Improvement

- Micromanages too many employee activities
- Has used threats to move employees to action
- Employee turnover rate higher than company average
- Employee sick time higher than average without reason
- Does not understand how to plan
- New hires often don't work out

Unacceptable

- Takes credit for accomplishments and blames others for problems
- Plans poorly and problems often occur as result
- Makes poor use of time, resources, and her staff
- Processes and procedures poorly organized
- Often runs into project crises because of weak management
- Work often finished late and over budget
- Has been subject of two successful grievances in the last year

Self-Monitoring/Self-Evaluation

- How do you think you did this year managing your staff? What do you think they thought of your management style and why?
- Tell me about some times when you thought your management skills were being challenged this year? How did you handle those times?
- How would you describe the approach you take to managing your staff?
- Describe some situations you encountered this year where you were particularly pleased with how you managed them.

Looking Forward

- You had some tough management situations this year. What can you do moving forward to minimize such situations?
- What management skills would you like to strengthen and what can I do to help you?
- Sometimes you're too easygoing about accepting some of what your staff does. How can you better exercise the management authority you have?
- I'd like you to develop a list of things you can do to become a more effective manager. Then let's set up a time to discuss them and work on a plan for you.

Managing Details

Outstanding

- Always is aware of and communicates details to others
- Extremely skilled at seeing and managing details
- Translates big picture to impact on details
- Breaks down problems into manageable details
- Makes sure the small things get done well

Exceeds Expectations

- Sees most details and attends to them as appropriate
- Does not get overwhelmed by details
- Keeps big picture in mind at all times
- Delegates details to the best people

Meets Expectations

- Knows when to tend to detail and when not to
- Communicates regularly with others involved in detail work
- Seeks help when overwhelmed
- Documents details so others can track and act accordingly

Needs Improvement

- Has been overwhelmed by details at times
- Sometimes loses track of things or misses steps
- Has missed some small yet important client requests
- Can't identify details of simple problems
- Stress levels rise as detail complexity increases

Unacceptable

- Quite often will forget to document essential details in handling customers' accounts
- Easily bored with small details
- Many details fall through cracks
- Short attention span causes problems
- Overwhelmed by more than simple details

Self-Monitoring/Self-Evaluation

- You've missed very few details this year and I want you to know I both notice and appreciate that. How do you manage to attend to all the details?

- Some significant details were missed at our last event. Why do you think that happened?

- Overall, how do you think you did last year managing all the details? Why?

- Compared with your colleagues, how do you think you manage the details and make sure things are wrapped up?

Looking Forward

- Some missed details this year led to some poor results for us. How can you contribute next year to making sure that details aren't missed?

- I'd like to see you use the computer more to manage details for all the projects you're involved in. There's a training program coming up in two weeks that I've enrolled you in and I know you'll find it to be of great benefit.

- How can I help you manage all the details you're responsible for?

Managing Expenses

Outstanding

- Looks for opportunities to reduce expenses
- Frequently suggests ideas to cut costs without sacrificing quality
- Did not exceed budget in any of last year's quarters
- Finds ways to eliminate unnecessary expenses
- Purchases only what is needed for success
- Sets priorities for spending to increase productivity

Exceeds Expectations

- Does not impede necessary small expenditures
- Spending has been within 2 percent of budget over the last three quarters
- Provides staff with reasonable spending authority
- Teaches staff to link spending with results
- Has developed new lower-cost methods now used in company

Meets Expectations

- Completes expenditure reports on time
- Stays within budget except for emergency situations
- Responds in a timely way to expenditure queries
- Seeks out cost-effective options

Needs Improvement

- Has made a few unnecessary purchases of equipment
- Chronically inflates expenses during planning
- Spending exceeded budget by 12 percent last year
- Expenses often exceed budget
- Takes a competitive attitude during budgeting

Unacceptable

- Return on investment for expenditures is low
- Has failed to meet two of the last four budgets

- Approves and makes purchases impulsively
- Lobbies for unneeded staff and money
- Has used money for purposes other than allocated

Self-Monitoring/Self-Evaluation

- How do you think you did in managing expenses this year? Why?
- Although you came in on budget overall, many of your projects came in at a far higher cost, and many at a far lower cost. Can you explain how you went about creating your project budgets?
- What were the major contributing factors for how you met your budget once again this year?
- What were the most difficult areas for you to control your expenses this past year? Why was that?

Looking Forward

- How can I help you manage your expenses better this year?
- You were off by quite a bit on a number of expenses this year. What can you suggest we do to get you closer this coming year?
- You hit the mark so well on your budget this year, I'd like you to speak with your colleagues at the upcoming management meeting about your secrets for success.
- I'd like to see you become more assertive in managing the expenses coming from your departments. What help can I offer you in this regard?

Mechanical Skills

Outstanding

- Without a doubt, the most talented mechanic we have
- Can fix every piece of machinery in the shop
- Works precisely, quickly, and safely
- Has engineered a number of improvements
- Excellent with preventive maintenance
- Effectively repairs intricate pieces of equipment
- An excellent troubleshooter

Exceeds Expectations

- Can troubleshoot a wide range of mechanical failures
- Repairs most devices without assistance
- Hasn't been stumped yet by a mechanical problem
- Spots failures/problems and resolves them quickly
- Consistently within time standards for jobs

Meets Expectations

- Able to repair most common problems with machinery
- An able and safe mechanic
- Competent at mechanical operations
- Usually able to find information to guide successful repairs
- Meets standards for mechanical procedures
- Shows ample strength and dexterity for the job
- Adequate eye-hand coordination

Needs Improvement

- Slow at troubleshooting
- Shortcuts in repairs have led to further downtime
- Lacks coordination to operate machine X
- He hurt himself three times last year, resulting in four days off the job
- Needs to improve understanding of the internal mechanism
- Mistakes hardware problems for software problems

Unacceptable

- Generally poor mechanical skills
- His machine was off-line 43 hours last year
- Works slowly and without regard for safety procedures
- Has sacrificed safety for quantity
- Needs oversight on most mechanical operations
- Unable to diagnose root cause for machine X's failure
- Unable to operate machine X after ___ months of training

Self-Monitoring/Self-Evaluation

- Mechanically speaking, how do you think you did this year? Why?
- Which machines do you find the easiest or most difficult to work on? Why?
- Which repair was the biggest challenge for you this year and what did it take for you to complete it?
- You seemed to have a difficult time getting up to speed working with our X machine. Is there something about it in particular that gave you an issue?
- How do you think you compare to your colleagues in mechanical skills?

Looking Forward

- What tools do you need to do your job more effectively?
- Please make up a list of seminars you'd like to attend to strengthen your mechanical skills. Then we'll discuss which ones our budget will allow you to attend.
- You were injured a couple of times last year and I know things were going on that made you lose focus. Everything seems back to normal now, but I wanted to ask if there's anything I can do to make it easier for you to focus on your machine.
- What repairs do you think you'll need to do this year? Do you have the tools and resources you need to complete them?

Multi-Tasking

Outstanding
- Effortlessly manages many projects at the same time
- Seamlessly shifts from one task to another
- Has met milestones for four major projects
- Managed $14.7 million worth of projects across three clients
- Uses project management software very effectively

Exceeds Expectations
- Can separate different aspects of her work very well
- Smoothly moves from one task to another and does all well
- Consistently maintains project logs for 13 projects
- Delegated high-level, challenging responsibilities to subordinates while maintaining oversight

Meets Expectations
- Ably handles multiple tasks
- Can move from one task to another competently
- Usually completes a variety of tasks within needed time frames
- Capable of coordinating two project teams' needs simultaneously

Needs Improvement
- Could strengthen concentration when working on many tasks
- Has fumbled one or two assignments requiring a number of tasks
- Forgets to do minor tasks that have cost us time later
- Capably coordinates one meeting, but can't handle two at the same time

Unacceptable
- Things often fall through the cracks when he/she has many responsibilities

- Loses focus when faced with even minor additional assignments
- Has walked out of the office on three occasions, frustrated with an average workload

Self-Monitoring/Self-Evaluation

- Your job requires you shift focus frequently. How well do you think you handle that?
- What were the most difficult times for you this past year in terms of multi-tasking? Why were they so challenging?
- You multi-task very well already. Can you think of ways you might do even better?
- You seem to lose focus when you shift from one task to another sometimes. What causes that?

Looking Forward

- How do you think you could manage all the tasks you have more effectively?
- What are some of the things you could do to multi-task better?
- How can I support you in managing all the details of all the projects you have responsibility for?
- We depend on you to manage many tasks. Is there anything you could use to make it easier on you?
- Would you be interested in attending a seminar on multi-tasking? You might pick up some things that would help.

Negotiating Skills

Outstanding
- Always negotiates successful win-win agreements
- Negotiated agreements that resulted in ___ new projects for company
- Contractees consistently positive about negotiation process
- Make no agreements that aren't in the company's interests
- Negotiated lower prices with three vendors, saving us $5 million last year
- Legal always signs off on agreements
- Takes into consideration the needs of all stakeholders

Exceeds Expectations
- Most negotiations go smoothly
- Legal seldom questions agreements
- Contractees happy with agreements
- Takes into consideration most contingencies
- Agreements she negotiated resulted in a 15 percent reduction in material costs

Meets Expectations
- Can be trusted to negotiate in our company's interests
- Makes use of legal advice during negotiation
- Informs superiors of progress on negotiations
- Takes others' views into account
- Suitably prepares for negotiations
- Uses reason rather than emotion in negotiations

Needs Improvement
- Does not adequately understand the give-and-take of negotiation
- Sometimes gets emotional during a negotiation
- Sometimes offers more than necessary to conclude negotiation
- Not well-prepared in some negotiation sessions

Unacceptable

- Consistently tries to take advantage of others
- Does not prepare for negotiation sessions
- Negotiations often result in losses for company
- Often gets emotional while negotiating
- Is unaware of contingencies in an agreement
- Agreements more often lose–lose than win–win

Self-Monitoring/Self-Evaluation

- I'd like you to think about all the negotiations you conducted this year—which stand out as the most successful and the least successful?
- Why you think some of your negotiations didn't work out as planned?
- What negotiating strategies did you employ that worked out well? How about those that didn't work out so well?
- What techniques did those you were negotiating with employ and were you able to counter them effectively?

Looking Forward

- What would help you negotiate more effectively?
- Do you think I could do more to help you prepare for negotiations? What additional support would you like from me?
- Would it be worth your while to attend a program on negotiating techniques? I'm sure we could find one that you'd get a lot out of.
- In which aspects of negotiating do you wish you were stronger? How might you go about developing them?

Organizational Skills

Outstanding

- Completed a major reorganization project this year
- We've received numerous compliments about her organizational skills
- Taught a mini-course on organizational skills last year
- Is always organized—her days, her projects, and her files

Exceeds Expectations

- Others can find things he organizes
- Excellent organization allows her to find what's needed right away
- Stays organized under high stress
- Keeps track of multiple things at once

Meets Expectations

- Keeps work space organized and functional
- Keeps well-organized files
- Can find needed information quickly
- Uses organizing tools well to save time and eliminate redundancies

Needs Improvement

- Requires a long time to find documents
- Filing system not easy for others to use
- Sometimes too concerned with neatness at the expense of good organization
- Intolerant of organizing approaches of others
- On a few occasions has been unable to find needed customer information

Unacceptable

- Has repeatedly failed to keep customer information current in files
- Has missed meetings due to disorganization

- Three customers commented last year on his inability to find needed information
- Often fails to file important documents
- Three critical pieces of information were misfiled last year and unable to be located

Self-Monitoring/Self-Evaluation

- How organized do you think you are? Can you give me some examples?
- What areas of your work are the best organized and which the worst? Why do you think there are differences?
- What do you think are the most difficult things to organize and why?
- You did so well organizing your work this year; to what do you attribute this?
- What have you noticed about how your coworkers keep track of things?

Looking Forward

- Looking back on the year, what things do you wish you had organized differently? How can you apply that knowledge moving forward?
- What tools or support can I offer you to help you stay more organized this coming year?
- What lessons have you learned about organizing that you think that some of your colleagues are unaware of? How about things they're doing that you're not?
- What can you do to ensure that vital details don't get missed again?

Orientation to Work

Outstanding
- Is very focused, knowledgeable, and dedicated to his work
- Consistently helps team members be more productive
- Toughest assignments completed with focus and dedication
- Has all the skills required for excellent work and uses them
- Have received many positive comments about how dedicated she is to her work

Exceeds Expectations
- Volunteers more than others
- Quick to learn from mistakes
- Interested in and dedicated to learning new things
- Concerned with team members' success

Meets Expectations
- Takes pride in work
- Balances needs of job and family effectively
- Treats customers well
- Always on time and at her desk ready to work

Needs Improvement
- Avoids leadership opportunities
- Sometimes anxious about new challenges
- Sometimes too cautious
- Easily distracted by nonwork issues
- Needs to do better making contingency plans

Unacceptable
- Seems uninterested in doing well
- Last to volunteer for work assignments
- Refuses to pitch in during emergencies
- Overly pessimistic
- Lacks skills required to perform acceptably
- Does not invest energy in learning to improve effectiveness

Self-Monitoring/Self-Evaluation

- Considering all the responsibilities I know you have outside of work, how do you think you did this year in contributing when we were low on resources? Can you give me an example?
- What is the thing that drives you most to do the work you do?
- How would you rate your level of focus and attention to your job?
- What responsibilities of yours are the easiest and what are the most difficult for you to manage? Why?

Looking Forward

- You've volunteered more than anyone else in the department and I really appreciate that. Do you have any thoughts of how we might get others to contribute as much?
- What can I do to help you get more energized about your work?
- I've noticed you slipping in the level of energy you have at work. Is there anything I can do to help?

Participative Management

Outstanding
- Knows when to delegate and not to delegate
- Inspires others to have confidence in themselves
- Identifies and uses employees' strengths and knowledge
- Understands own limitations and calls on others to help
- Open to criticism and uses it to improve her approach

Exceeds Expectations
- His employees are always comfortable making suggestions
- Engenders a strong participative orientation in her department
- Gets staff input for major decisions
- Helps staff understand the company's business
- Provides open-door access that employees use

Meets Expectations
- Delegates, then does not meddle
- Asks for others' opinions about approaches whenever practical
- Treats employee input seriously
- Provides needed information to staff
- Rewards staff for good ideas

Needs Improvement
- Pretends to delegate, but stays too involved
- Sometimes defensive
- Prefers autocratic style
- Staff hesitant to approach with ideas

Unacceptable
- His employees are afraid to become involved or contribute ideas
- Intimidates staff
- Asks for suggestions, then ignores them

- Takes credit for her employees' ideas
- Her negative attitude undermines cooperation among employees

Self-Monitoring/Self-Evaluation

- How much involvement do you think your employees feel they have in managing their own work?
- What were the issues you had this year deciding when to delegate and to whom you should delegate?
- Do you think you'd see different results from your team if you involved them earlier on?
- Your project with X went so well. How did you manage that?

Looking Forward

- I think you learned this year that you can't do it all yourself! How have you been doing with delegating and involving your team more? What would you like to continue to develop this coming year?
- What have you been doing to develop your participative management skills? What are you planning for future development?
- Some have mentioned that you don't seem to trust them and that you're reluctant to share responsibility for projects. How can you turn this view around?
- How do you plan to involve your group more in the day-to-day management of operations?

Personal Growth

Outstanding
- Balances work and family/outside interests
- Attended three work-related seminars on her personal time
- Independently pursues opportunities to learn
- Invests a lot of time outside of work gaining job knowledge
- Has pursued and maintains excellent mentor relationships

Exceeds Expectations
- Dramatic improvement in maturity over the last year
- Improved stress management ability this year
- Participated in a number of community development projects
- Seeks to improve understanding of diverse people
- Helps others with personal growth

Meets Expectations
- Seeks help as needed
- Assumes responsibility for her own successes and failures
- Regularly asks for feedback and responds by making an effort to improve
- Sees problems as opportunities to learn

Needs Improvement
- Overly sensitive to negative feedback
- Seems to have reached a "growth plateau"
- Goes into denial when faced with personal problems
- His work has been negatively impacted by personal issues several times this year

Unacceptable
- Denies existence of personal difficulties
- Refuses needed help
- Has unresolved substance abuse problems
- Prone to self-deception

- Work suffers because of her inability to balance work, family, and outside interests

Self-Monitoring/Self-Evaluation

- I've seen you do a lot this year to develop yourself. Which things made the biggest difference?
- How are you progressing in developing your potential within our organization? How do you think others view your growth?
- There's been a lot you've had to manage this year between work and your personal life; how are you doing with that now?
- What things are interfering with your self-development?

Looking Forward

- Have you established any specific goals for your personal development this year?
- What challenges do you think will be the greatest for you this coming year? What can I do to help you handle them?
- I've seen little effort on your part to balance work with your family life. I know family is very important, but work is too. I'd like to talk about how you can keep your priorities balanced and focus better on work and minimize personal distractions while on the job.
- You should be proud of what you've accomplished this year, managing your role here with that as a mother and soccer coach, and with neither role interfering with the other. Have you been able to plan so this coming year should be more of the same? What is your plan?

Persuasiveness

Outstanding

- Very persuasive in all interactions—with coworkers, superiors, and customers
- Understands and believes in the problem-solving approach in convincing others
- Makes excellent use of "shared benefits" to influence others
- Makes sales others cannot
- Others leave believing idea was their own

Exceeds Expectations

- Is persuasive in even the most difficult of "sales"
- Anticipates others' needs and wants
- Modifies communication to reach different audiences
- Excellent delivery of persuasive messages
- Effective in responding to objections
- Speaks with power, confidence, and knowledge
- Confident speaking to large groups

Meets Expectations

- Justifies positions logically and persuasively
- Uses supporting information when persuading others
- Can adequately answer question
- Does not oversell
- Writes coherent, persuasive documents as needed
- Often succeeds in persuading others to follow particular course of action

Needs Improvement

- Is sometimes timid when communicating with others
- Doesn't realize merits of own ideas
- Not always aware of how he comes across
- Lacks some large group speaking skills
- Starts strong but gets thrown by resistance or objections in meetings and presentations

Unacceptable

- Uses threats and coercion to persuade others
- Received a number of complaints about heavy-handedness
- Has been described as a bully
- Perceived as wanting "own way"
- Gives up much too easily and doesn't bother to convince others to do something a desired way

Self-Monitoring/Self-Evaluation

- You did very well in a number of situations where you needed to be persuasive. How do you think you've done overall? Can you give me an example?
- You weren't able to convince client X to upgrade. What do you think was going on there? Might you have used another tactic?
- Which were the toughest "persuasive" discussions you had this year? What approach did you take? How might you have handled them differently?
- There are times when others see you as a bully. How about as too passive? What can you do about that perception?

Looking Forward

- How might you find a balance between being overly aggressive at times and too passive at other times?
- There are a number of things I think you could learn to sell more persuasively. I'd like you to spend a couple of days with John Smith, one of our most effective salespeople, and see what you pick up.
- Are there things that I can do to help you prepare better for some of your more challenging communications?
- I've prepared a little exercise for you. Next week, you're going to come in and try to sell me on doing X, and I'm going to do my best to be a tough customer. Be prepared, and I will be, as well.

Phone Skills

Outstanding

- Effectively calms angry callers with tact and professionalism
- Smooth and calm under pressure
- Volume of calls handled consistently exceeds standards
- Handles high volume of calls with ease
- Advises staff on handling tough calls
- Callers call back and request him/her

Exceeds Expectations

- Has received numerous compliments from clients
- Quickly deals with angry callers and moves on to the next call without hesitation
- Always takes phone messages accurately and professionally
- Transfers calls smoothly and accurately
- Sounds cheerful even when overloaded with other work

Meets Expectations

- Checks back with callers on hold every few minutes while problem-solving
- Answers all calls within four rings
- Consistently returns calls within the time frame promised
- Consistently meets call volume standard
- Keeps promises regarding returning calls
- Updates voice mail message at least once a day as required

Needs Improvement

- Sometimes sounds rushed to customers
- Lacks understanding of phone equipment
- Frequently handles fewer calls than expected
- Leaves incomplete or inaccurate telephone messages for others at times
- Uncomfortable using voice mail
- Sometimes sounds impatient or flustered with others on the phone

Unacceptable

- Customers often hang up due to wait
- Complaints received about poor phone manners
- Lost at least three sales due to phone interactions
- Often does not return calls
- Hangs up abruptly
- Frequently becomes too informal with callers
- Receives too many requests from callers to speak to management

Self-Monitoring/Self-Evaluation

- Overall, how would you rate your phone skills? Why?
- Which are the toughest calls for you to handle? Why?
- What techniques do you find yourself using most often to handle difficult customers? Can you give me an example?
- Some customers say that you seem distracted while on the phone. Why do you think that is?

Looking Forward

- What phone skills do you want to develop in the coming year?
- Since our call volume has increased dramatically, we'll be getting a new phone system. We'll have trainers come in and teach you how to use it the week after next. How do you feel about a new phone system and training?
- I know there are times that customers can really get to you, but you've got to show less frustration with them. How might you go about doing that?
- Can you think of ways you can remain professional on the phone but yet move customers along with their orders more quickly?
- What can we do to improve our phone communications in general? Is there anything I could do to help you improve your communication skills?

Physical Abilities

Outstanding

- Paces himself so he never seems to become fatigued
- Performs all physical aspects of job flawlessly
- Exceedingly agile
- Unloaded 75 50-lb. bags without stopping once
- Makes sure actions are always performed safely
- Can lift ___ pounds above job requirement

Exceeds Expectations

- Rarely misses work due to illness
- Through exercise and diet, he keeps himself in shape for the physical demands of the job
- Excellent depth perception
- Moves quickly without sacrificing safety
- Good dexterity and feel for all things mechanical

Meets Expectations

- Strong enough to meet job requirements
- Sufficient stamina to meet job requirements
- Can lift 40 pounds as per job requirement
- Shows good situational awareness around shop floor
- Understands and respects own limitations

Needs Improvement

- Becomes uncoordinated under stress
- Lacks some fine motor skills
- Sometimes drops tools
- Has difficulty lifting 30-lb. boxes

Unacceptable

- Safety risk due to clumsiness
- Prone to injury on the job
- Physically unfit for job demands

- Has injured himself three times due to improper lifting procedures
- Comes to work physically unready (for example, not enough rest)

Self-Monitoring/Self-Evaluation

- Compared to others, do you think you "pull your own weight"? How?
- You strained your back last month—has it been OK since then? What are you doing to employ proper lifting techniques?
- What have you been doing to ensure you're physically able to handle our work?
- Do you think you're in better or worse shape since you've started working here? Can you give me an example?

Looking Forward

- Of all the work you have to do, which do you find the most strenuous? What can you do to minimize the strain?
- You've had some difficulty handling the physical aspects of your work this year. What are your plans for getting in shape?
- You've missed loading quotas a few times this year, yet most times you make them. Why do you think you've missed these quotas? What will you do to improve in the coming year?
- We've made arrangements with a local fitness club to offer substantial discounts for memberships to our employees. Are you interested in becoming a member?

Planning and Scheduling

Outstanding

- Always has contingency plans to overcome delays caused by others
- Copes well with problems beyond her control
- Helps others stay organized and on time
- Others regularly rely on his scheduling abilities
- Excellent at planning and scheduling even the minutest detail

Exceeds Expectations

- Does not overcommit herself or her staff
- Has never created scheduling conflicts
- Plans are consistently practical and doable
- Anticipates where schedules can go wrong and plans accordingly

Meets Expectations

- Develops both long- and short-term plans
- Anticipates needs of project effectively
- Uses planning tools effectively
- Makes use of automated scheduling tools

Needs Improvement

- Can't see big picture in planning
- Doesn't consult others when required
- Misses details when planning and scheduling
- Leaves planning until last minute
- Failed to schedule a conference room for a large customer presentation

Unacceptable

- Cannot schedule for others
- His plans and schedules often need to be returned for revision

- Fails to plan for easily foreseeable contingencies
- Neglects to tell others of schedule changes

Self-Monitoring/Self-Evaluation

- In planning and scheduling this year, how do you think you did? Can you give me an example?
- You missed some critical deadlines earlier in the year. What have you been doing differently since then?
- What information sources do you typically use to guide you in your planning and scheduling?
- Which of the projects you worked on this year do you feel were best planned? Why do you think the planning went as well as it did?

Looking Forward

- In what ways can you improve your planning and scheduling this year?
- What can I do to help you more effectively plan or schedule your projects?
- Based on what you learned this past year about how to plan and schedule, what will you do differently this coming year?

Political Skills

Outstanding

- She's adept at coordinating diverse groups to work together toward a common goal
- Lobbies effectively for our interests with both clients and vendors
- Politically astute
- Uses power with discretion
- Exceptionally skilled at dealing with people at all levels of the organization
- Exceptionally skilled at choosing when to follow and when to lead

Exceeds Expectations

- Influences others with information, tact, and diplomatic skills
- Accepts superiors' use of power graciously
- Gets along well with people with diverse needs in many different situations
- Understands and works with the political climate of our clients
- Can be trusted to handle politically sensitive situations
- Isn't intimidated by titles or others' power

Meets Expectations

- Compromises effectively when needed
- Respects others' positions in organization
- Sensitive to and works well with office politics
- Seeks to minimize politics when possible
- Accepts prerogative of executive to decide issues
- Is able to work the politics of our organization

Needs Improvement

- Has overstepped "political lines" at times
- Argues trivial points to the detriment of achieving goals
- Seen as difficult by others

- Wields power unnecessarily
- Sometimes unaware of politically sensitive situations
- Often in conflict with peers

Unacceptable

- Often oversteps authority and others' toes
- Speaks without regard for others' reactions
- Made a number of politically insensitive remarks about other departments
- Questions authority without valid reasons
- Doesn't work well with superiors
- Unaware of political implications of most situations

Self-Monitoring/Self-Evaluation

- Overall, how do you think you do politically with the team? Can you give me an example?
- You seem to almost always get along with people while getting things done your way. How do you do that?
- Tell me about some times you know you "ruffled some feathers" around here. What was going on? What did you do? What would you do differently if you knew then what you know now?
- How did you manage to turn Frank around from an opponent to an ally?
- You show very little deference to those in higher authority. Why is that?

Looking Forward

- Dave is one of our most experienced in managing the political environment around here. I'd like you to work with him for a few days next week and see what you can pick up. We'll talk about it some more afterwards. Are you OK with that?
- What can you do to improve your ability to connect with and influence others better?

- There have been times when you've backed off your position because you perceived others to have more authority than you. How can I help you stick with your position despite who's opposed to it?
- Some have commented that you seem too political. What do you think about that? What do you think an appropriate response to comments like that should be?

Potential for Advancement

Outstanding
- Effective leader without formal power
- Has stood in for supervisor without problems
- Eager for new challenges
- Has undertaken formal study for advancement
- Learns quickly and in depth
- By attitude and skills she has shown potential to advance to high levels in the organization

Exceeds Expectations
- Quickly mastered current job
- Often helps solve others' problems
- Developed skills and abilities without prompting
- Pursues independent self-development

Meets Expectations
- Learns effectively over time
- Does current job acceptably
- Willing to go extra mile

Needs Improvement
- Learns slowly
- Repeats past solutions even when inappropriate
- Unaware of areas that need improvement
- Would require coaching in supervisory skills

Unacceptable
- Does not seem to have the capability to rise above current position
- Has not generated the confidence of others required for promotion
- Cannot see this employee in higher levels
- Cannot cope with complex decision-making

Self-Monitoring/Self-Evaluation

- How do you think your potential for advancement has been changed by your work this past year?
- In the past year, what have you done with regard to your long-term goals with this company?
- You took on many large projects this year with an advanced level of responsibility. How did you like that?
- Tell me about the biggest challenge you faced this year at work and what you did to meet it. What do you think of the results you got?

Looking Forward

- What could you do to increase your advancement potential this coming year?
- I think you're ready to take on more responsibility this year. If you agree, let's talk about which projects you think you'd be well suited for.
- You haven't shown the level of leadership I think you're capable of within your team. I think that gap will hold you back. Are you interested in attending a seminar to strengthen your skills and increase your potential for advancement within our division?
- What can I do to help you increase your advancement potential in this organization?

Problem-Solving

Outstanding
- Highly proficient and creative at solving problems
- Identifies problems in own area and develops resourceful solutions
- Weighs cost/benefit of many solutions to a problem
- Always addresses root causes in solutions
- Anticipates problems and solves them before they develop
- Analyzes problems thoroughly and takes appropriate action

Exceeds Expectations
- Recognizes similarities among situations and appropriately addresses them
- Thorough in analyzing and developing solutions
- Knows when a problem warrants solving
- Always makes recommendations when a problem surfaces
- Develops alternative solutions to problems

Meets Expectations
- Satisfactory problem-solving skills
- Can analyze facts, information, and evidence logically
- Solutions to problems go beyond surface causes
- Recommends solutions to problems
- Sometimes will anticipate problems
- Uses good judgment and information in solving problems

Needs Improvement
- Generates solutions that don't always solve problems
- Knows solutions but doesn't recommend them
- Fails to identify underlying or systemic problems
- Fails to completely analyze problems
- Doesn't recognize trends in recurring problems

Unacceptable

- Has insufficient problem-solving skills
- Weak problem-analysis skills
- Solutions address only surface problems
- Finds problems but doesn't solve them
- Doesn't generate solutions for problems
- Lets others find and fix problems

Self-Monitoring/Self-Evaluation

- How do you think you did this year with regard to problem-solving? Can you give me some examples of successful problem-solving?
- Which were the most difficult problems for which you had to find a solution? What was so difficult about them? How did you come up with the solution?
- It seems you have a tough time coming up with solutions for some of our customers' problems. Why do you think that is?
- What process do you go through when faced with a tough problem?

Looking Forward

- What have you learned this year about problem-solving that you will apply in the future?
- What issues do you see in our department with the way we solve customer problems? What do you think we could do to be more effective at it?
- What can I do to make it easier on you to solve problems quickly and effectively?
- I'd like to see you break large problems down into component pieces so you don't become intimidated by the scale of the problem. Could we apply this approach together on your next problem?

Product Knowledge

Outstanding
- In-depth knowledge of all products
- Can explain product benefits to customers in ways that always address their problems
- Consistently recommends the best product for our customer
- Often praised by customers for her expertise
- Makes it a point to keep up-to-date on competitors' products
- Knows all the technical specifications of all our products
- Confidently translates features to benefits for customers

Exceeds Expectations
- Knowledgeable about most products
- Customers request advice about products from him often
- Has received positive comments from customers
- Makes suggestions to improve product line
- Familiar with competitors' products

Meets Expectations
- Familiar with product line
- Gives credible product descriptions to most customers
- Demonstrates proper use of product
- Effectively troubleshoots product problems

Needs Improvement
- Superficial knowledge of most products
- Often needs help explaining some products to customers
- Customers sometimes ask to speak to someone more expert
- Ineffective teacher on use of product
- Often relies on customer's expertise

Unacceptable
- Lacks critical product knowledge
- Presents incorrect product information to customers

- Loses sales as a result of lack of knowledge
- Almost never matches customer need with proper product

Self-Monitoring/Self-Evaluation

- Do you feel comfortable with your knowledge of all our products? What can we do to improve your knowledge?
- Which products do you wish you understood better?
- What would you say are the key benefits for customers using our product X? Describe the benefits of product Y.
- How often would you say that you're not sure what product to recommend to a customer? Why?

Looking Forward

- Of all the product knowledge training programs you've been to, which were the best? Why?
- I've seen you struggle trying to translate a customer's needs into a specific product recommendation. I'd like you to enroll in all our product training sessions.
- Which products are the most difficult for you and your colleagues to understand and explain?
- What can you do to learn more about our products this coming year?

Programming Skills

Outstanding
- Others can easily understand and alter her code written
- Instructs and helps other programmers
- Has developed innovative ways to reduce computer load
- Solicits feedback on own work

Exceeds Expectations
- Creates excellently documented code
- Creates tight, efficient code
- Works well with minimum supervision
- Provides suggestions to analysts when needed
- Can work long hours when required to finish project

Meets Expectations
- Follows company standards for coding
- Formats code well
- Debugs his own code well before sending it on
- Competent in needed programming languages
- Follows system analyst's specifications
- Clarifies specifications when needed

Needs Improvement
- Documentation sparse or difficult to understand
- Confuses programming with system analysis
- He programs accurately but slowly
- Lacks depth of understanding of programming languages
- Needs upgrading in program testing

Unacceptable
- Changes code without telling anyone
- Alters program specifications without consulting client
- Code has many bugs
- Consistently misses deadlines
- Has caused project delays in past year

- Has difficulty working with [programming language]
- Has not improved in last two years

Self-Monitoring/Self-Evaluation

- Which programs were the most difficult for you to code and why?
- A number of your programs had to be debugged repeatedly. What process do you use to test your own programs?
- How do you think you've done this year with your programming? Can you give me some examples?
- What applications do you find the easiest to work with? How about the most difficult?

Looking Forward

- What languages do you want to develop greater knowledge of this coming year?
- What suggestions do you have to help us all become more proficient at programming?
- I'd like to see you improve your error rate this year. What would it take to accomplish that?
- You're so good at working with our programs' code. Would you be willing to lead a session with your colleagues on the best practices you follow?

Project Management

Outstanding
- Understands the nuances of project planning
- Has complete mastery of Microsoft Project
- Brings projects in consistently below budget and on or ahead of schedule
- Knows how to select the best team to undertake a project
- Superior at coordinating resources needed to complete a project
- Communicates well with all project team members so problems don't occur
- Successfully dealt with five difficult problems that could have stalled project
- Interacts effectively with all stakeholders in project

Exceeds Expectations
- Makes effective use of Gantt and PERT charts
- Meets project budgets and time frames
- Has communication system for keeping all project team members informed
- Accurately estimates project budgets
- Developed systems for keeping projects on track
- Effectively brings projects to closure

Meets Expectations
- Works well with project team members
- Effectively deals with problems when they arise
- Effectively uses project planning tools
- Projects usually come in no more than 5 percent over budget

Needs Improvement
- Does not fully understand project planning tools
- Materials arrive at project either too early or too late
- Team members sometimes complain they are not fully informed

- Three projects came in ___ percent over budget
- The needs of external stakeholders are not always considered

Unacceptable
- Project time frames frequently are not met
- Steps in projects have been poorly planned, resulting in wasted resources and time
- Cannot understand how to use Microsoft Project
- Did not select the right people for the project team
- Two projects came in more than 25 percent over budget

Self-Monitoring/Self-Evaluation
- Overall, how would you rate your project management skills this past year?
- What aspects of project management did you find the most challenging? Which are the easiest? Why?
- Of all the projects you handled this year, which do you think went the best? Which was the most problematic? Why?
- When you need to dedicate resources for a project, how do you go about deciding which project gets which resources?

Looking Forward
- Although some of your projects came in on time and on budget, a few did not. How can you better manage project budgets going forward?
- Which aspects of project management would you like to develop this year? How would you like to go about doing that?
- What have you learned this year from the many projects you've been involved with?
- You seem to be uncomfortable with our project management software. There's a seminar coming up that I'd like you to attend. Do you think that would be a good investment of your time?

Quality Management

Outstanding

- Conscious of customer requirements and makes sure defect-free products are always delivered
- Quality controls established to deliver only 99.9 percent defect-free outputs
- Has all processes documented
- Conscientiously practices continuous improvement of processes
- Developed training course that resulted in all line personnel using statistical process control (SPC) to improve processes
- Rework and scrap costs reduced by ___ percent

Exceeds Expectations

- Rarely loses focus on quality
- Continuous improvement is a constant focus
- Consistently meets goals for costs and quality of outputs
- Uses SPC to measure and improve processes
- Shares information and resources to help others improve
- An effective advocate of SPC
- Had only a ___ percent defect rate
- Has delivered accurately and on time to 23 clients requesting samples

Meets Expectations

- Quality of outputs meets standards
- Practices quality control techniques
- Has good SPC techniques
- Understands how to analyze and improve processes
- Defect rates meet company standards
- Understands how to analyze and improve processes
- Takes customer needs into consideration in work
- Makes wise use of resources

Needs Improvement

- Does not have adequate understanding of SPC techniques
- The defect rate in some processes is unacceptable
- XYZ project was ___ percent over budget because of errors
- His scrap and rework costs exceeded budget by ___ percent
- On three occasions, colleagues had to redo work
- Customers returned ___ percent of packages missing parts

Unacceptable

- Defects greatly exceed standards
- Does not understand or practice SPC
- Makes errors frequently in his work
- Production runs averaged a 70 percent acceptance rate
- Wastes resources

Self-Monitoring/Self-Evaluation

- How do you think you did managing quality this year?
- Your 4 percent reject rate is high. What factors do you think contributed to that?
- What did you do this year to involve everyone in taking responsibility for product quality?
- List the factors that you think advanced the quality of your work. Which factors caused it to be reduced?

Looking Forward

- What have you concluded needs to be done this year to increase the quality of work your departments produce?
- Tell me about the changes you're planning on making to reduce your reject rate this year.
- You've had excellent control over quality this year and I want to make sure that continues next year. What can I do to help?
- I'd like you to involve your team members more in managing quality. How could you do that?
- I'd like you to attend an SPC seminar so you can apply it more rigorously to our production process. Are you interested in that?

Quality of Work

Outstanding
- Work is consistently error-free
- Takes special precautions to prevent errors
- She consistently receives praise for her work quality
- Other employees use his work as a model
- Customers regularly compliment her work

Exceeds Expectations
- Leads our group in error reduction
- She's received commendations from five customers
- Work is regularly completed on time and error-free
- Output quality makes it easy for others to do their jobs
- Focuses on continuous quality improvement

Meets Expectations
- Work is regularly error-free
- Quality of work meets standards
- Seeks training to learn how to improve quality
- Works well with customers to assure quality
- Makes use of quality improvement techniques
- Works well with other employees to ensure quality

Needs Improvement
- Employees complain about the quality of his work
- Mistakes caused work stoppage on two occasions
- She does not pay enough attention to quality issues
- Needs to focus on reducing error rate
- He needs to apply the training he received to improve quality of outputs

Unacceptable
- On five occasions, errors caused work stoppage
- Defects in outputs caused one customer to choose another vendor

- Does not understand how to improve quality of outputs
- Quality is not a priority for him

Self-Monitoring/Self-Evaluation

- The quality of work you produced this year increased (decreased) over last year. To what do you attribute that? Why?
- I'm not sure you think that your error rate is high, but it's the highest in our division. How do you check the quality of your work before you pass it on?
- What would help you get to a 100 percent quality rating?
- Can you recall earlier this year when the quality of your work dropped significantly? What did you do to turn that around?

Looking Forward

- What could you do to improve the quality of your work this coming year?
- Are there things I could do on my end to help you deliver a higher quality product?
- What do you plan to do to bring the quality of your work up to standard?
- I know you care a lot about the quality of your work, but you spend too much time checking and not enough producing. What might you do to still check your work but deliver more quality?

Quantity of Work

Outstanding
- Consistently meets or exceeds production targets
- Helps others achieve their targets
- Diagnoses barriers to producing desired quantities
- Fixes problems and barriers to hitting targets
- In top 5 percent in sales each month

Exceeds Expectations
- Exceeded target by __ percent last year
- Effective at dealing with obstacles
- Suggested ways for everyone to increase quantity of output
- Contributes to profit margin

Meets Expectations
- Ordinarily achieves targets
- Produces well without slowing others down
- Takes on challenge of difficult quotas
- Produces __ items per month

Needs Improvement
- 10 percent below target last year
- Lacks a few skills needed to increase production
- Hasn't volunteered for skill upgrade courses
- Output sometimes affected when under stress

Unacceptable
- Interferes with coworkers' production
- Unwilling to learn how to improve
- Seriously below production targets last year
- Doesn't show concern for missing targets

Self-Monitoring/Self-Evaluation
- You've done exceptionally well this year in terms of the quantity of your work. Why is it so much improved over last year?

- Can you explain why half the time I come into your area you're talking with a coworker and not working?
- In looking at your production figures, I noticed that they range quite widely around our production standards. What accounts for this variability?
- Why are you producing less than those with less experience than you?

Looking Forward

- I'd like to talk about how often you're getting interrupted by your coworkers with questions and come up with some ideas for you to minimize these interruptions.
- Your drive for quality of work is hurting the quantity you produce. What can you do to deliver the same quality while increasing production?
- Given how well you've delivered both quality and quantity of work this year, what could others do to produce like you?
- Given your experience with our new production standards, what do you think would be a reasonably challenging goal for you this coming year?
- I'd like you to spend time this week working with your coworkers on the line. For those who work slower than you, please suggest things they can do to improve their quantity. From those who are faster than you, I'd like you to pick up techniques you can use.

Research Abilities

Outstanding

- Zeros in on essential information quickly and effectively
- Can find almost anything online whenever needed
- Consistently prepared with information before needed
- Excellent at reconciling conflicting information
- Accurately interprets complex statistical data

Exceeds Expectations

- Finds needed information quickly
- Displays very good Internet research skills
- Evaluates contradictory information
- Determines relative importance of information
- Ferrets out difficult-to-find information

Meets Expectations

- Completes assigned research projects on time
- "Googles" with alacrity
- Prepares research reports on time
- Understands and makes use of technical papers in his field
- Sets realistic deadlines for gathering information

Needs Improvement

- Doesn't use all research tools available
- Needs to improve use of keywords in searching
- Sometimes suffers information overload
- Reports research findings in confusing way
- Cannot research outside of specialized field

Unacceptable

- Mistakes trivial information for important
- Incapable of finding needed information on the Internet
- Does not distinguish between the wheat and the chaff
- Conclusions often muddy the waters
- Consistently misinterprets data

Self-Monitoring/Self-Evaluation

- What do you see as your greatest strengths and weaknesses in your research skills?
- Which research project was the most difficult or challenging for you this year? Why do you think that was?
- Let's talk about how you came to the conclusion that the X market would be a weak one for us to move into.

Looking Forward

- Because your research skills are so critical to your role here, I've scheduled you to attend a seminar next month to strengthen your skills.
- You have often missed essential pieces of information while doing competitive research. What have you learned that you'll apply to the research you conduct this year?
- What would help you conduct your research more effectively?
- When I give you assignments, do you feel you have enough information to conduct effective research?

Resource Use

Outstanding
- Creates excellent return on investment
- Consistently applies the proper resources where they're needed
- Excellent resource forecaster
- Has introduced many cost-saving measures
- Uses innovative ways to save

Exceeds Expectations
- Works within budget and allocated personnel
- Required more resources only due to emergency
- Suggests ways to save money and resources
- Considers various ways to complete jobs with lower costs

Meets Expectations
- Coordinates resource use with others
- Rarely needs overtime to get jobs done
- Returns resources so others can use
- Treats resources carefully

Needs Improvement
- Takes resources without informing others
- Has assigned the wrong people to projects
- Uses resources designated for others
- Consistently underanticipates resources needed
- Sometimes forgets others may need same resources

Unacceptable
- Rarely comes in on budget
- Assigns people for projects based on availability, not skills necessary
- Negatively impacts others' work
- Received complaints about hoarding resources
- Has damaged resources needed by others

Self-Monitoring/Self-Evaluation

- Overall, how do you think you've done with managing resources this year?

- There were a few times last year when you didn't have the resources you needed to complete a project on time. What will you do to ensure this doesn't happen again?

- How do you decide which projects get which resources?

- Do you think you're getting the resources you need to fulfill your responsibilities? What can you do in cases where you're not getting access to adequate resources?

Looking Forward

- You got caught short on resources on a couple of significant occasions last year. What are you doing to plan ahead better?

- How can you utilize resources more effectively? Do you foresee any obstacles to your doing those things this coming year?

- How can I help you plan your resource use better?

- What ideas do you have to help our department manage our resources more effectively?

Outstanding

- Always adheres to safety rules and procedures
- Has had no safety infractions
- Wears appropriate safety gear on shop floor at all times
- Tolerates no safety violations
- Monitors employees' safety practices at least one hour every day
- Always reminds staff of safety issues at the morning meeting

Exceeds Expectations

- Has an excellent safety record
- Encourages safe practices often
- Makes safety a high priority on all tasks
- Her team had only one minor accident during hazardous work
- Enforces safety very strictly

Meets Expectations

- Performs all work within safety guidelines
- Has a good safety record
- A safe worker
- Values safe working procedures
- Strictly maintains vehicle according to maintenance manual

Needs Improvement

- Uses safety equipment only when told
- Failed to wear safety goggles twice in the last quarter
- Missed work three times owing to unsafe practices and injuries resulting from them
- Does not enforce safety practices among employees
- Fails to adhere to safe work practices
- Sacrifices safety for productivity

Unacceptable

- Has violated safety guidelines many times
- Failed to adhere to safety rules ___ times in one month
- Ignores safety rules
- Tolerates unsafe or hazardous conditions
- Repeatedly ignores "no smoking" signs
- Frequently does not wear safety equipment

Self-Monitoring/Self-Evaluation

- You know how critical safety practices are for us. What have you done in your area to reinforce safety requirements?
- You've been among our safest employees—year after year without any incident. Then last year, you had three accidents. Is that just a coincidence or are things going on that are distracting you from working safely?
- How often would you say you sidestep safety regulations? Why?
- What are some of the changes you've made to address the safety concerns we've spoken about on other occasions?

Looking Forward

- I've seen a number of times where safety devices were removed from machines by the operators so they could meet quota more easily. What steps are you going to take to ensure this doesn't continue?
- What, if any, safety requirements would you say we need to add, or for those we already have, to reinforce better?
- You strained your back three times last year from improper lifting techniques and we spoke about that each time. What is it that I need to say or do to make sure you lift properly in the future?
- We need to improve our safety record considerably over last year. What ideas do you have to contribute to this effort?

Sales Ability

Outstanding

- Is among our finest sales representatives
- Has closed all our large sales
- A role model for other salespeople
- Always makes the sales target
- Closed 33 percent of sales when she was called in as a product specialist
- Exceeded sales target by 23 percent
- Successfully leveraged our success with company X to have it try our latest version of product Z
- Powerful opening and closing presentations
- Clearly understands clients' needs

Exceeds Expectations

- Maintains excellent relations with clients
- Very good opening presentations
- Always closes with some action for prospect to take
- Represents our company very well
- Comes across as an educator more than a sales representative—and this works well!
- Introduced product X to three new markets—auto, computer, and appliance
- Her clients referred three other companies to us, citing her excellent service
- Great closer!
- Sends birthday, anniversary, holiday cards to clients and their staff

Meets Expectations

- A dedicated salesperson
- Consistently makes sales quota
- Rarely misses sales quota
- Could become a very good salesperson soon

- Persuades more often than not
- Stocks car with appropriate samples on a weekly basis for all upcoming calls
- Successfully had our product specifications included in prospect X's request for proposal (RFP)
- Maintains folders with newspaper articles and clippings for each account and delivers them on the sales call
- Good product knowledge, but weak on closing

Needs Improvement
- Is below his assigned quota by 5 percent
- Needs to learn a lot more about our products
- Needs to learn more about sales techniques
- Is uncomfortable presenting to large client groups
- Maintains good relations with prospects, but doesn't close effectively

Unacceptable
- Met only 80 percent of quota
- Knows few sales techniques
- Has weak relationships with clients
- Sales ability is very poor
- Needs to improve sales in area of responsibility immediately

Self-Monitoring/Self-Evaluation
- What would you say were the most significant factors accounting for your making (not making) your sales target this year?
- If you could strengthen one or two aspects of your sales ability, what would they be?
- Which were among the most difficult sales you made this year? Why were they so tough?
- You seem to have developed great loyalty among your customers. How did you do it?
- Which of the techniques that you learned at the last sales training session do you find the most difficult to use?

Looking Forward

- Although you've always completed your allotted number of sales contacts, your sales are below where they should be. What will you do to increase your sales this coming year?

- I'd like you to spend a week with our number one rep in Boston and study him in action. He consistently exceeds our targets, and I want you to learn how he does it.

- What support can I offer you to help you increase your sales figures?

- What suggestions do you have for our organization to increase its sales? I'd like to see you champion some of those ideas and put them into practice this year.

- You seem to have excellent product knowledge, but just are not closing sales. What issues have you run into that prevented you from calling for the sale? What can you do to be more assertive in the call to action?

Supervisory Skills

Outstanding
- Exceptionally dedicated and sensitive to employee needs
- Actions have resulted in strong staff loyalty
- Excellent mentor to employees
- Provides excellent and regular feedback to employees
- Has mastery of all staff jobs
- Excellent team leader
- Successfully removes obstacles that get in staff's way
- Has the loyalty and support of staff

Exceeds Expectations
- Supervises staff with skill
- Excellent staff motivator
- Lays out projects clearly for staff
- Assigns job responsibilities to challenge and develop her staff
- Provides opportunities for staff to develop
- Understands work flow and technologies used

Meets Expectations
- Appropriately trains staff
- Explains new projects clearly to reduce errors
- Delegates when appropriate
- Keeps management informed
- Acknowledges and rewards good performances
- Sets goals with staff

Needs Improvement
- Occasionally heavy-handed
- Poor planning results in staff overload
- Tends to restrict learning opportunities
- Could listen more to staff

Unacceptable
- Frequently critical of staff
- Avoids communicating with staff

- Staff shows little respect for person or position
- Hoards information
- Has had more than one legitimate grievance filed
- Does not respect confidentiality issues
- Always uses command-and-control approach

Self-Monitoring/Self-Evaluation

- How do you think your staff rated you on overall supervisory skills? How about some of the specifics—where do you think you were viewed well or not so well?
- Of all the supervisory challenges you faced this year, which was the greatest challenge? What did you do to meet it? How did it turn out?
- You did an excellent job of developing many of your employees this year, but three of them left our organization. Why do you think that was? What might you have done differently to retain them?
- When you assign work, what factors do you consider when deciding who should do what?

Looking Forward

- You seem to have some issues with communicating the big picture to your teams and they aren't focused clearly on specific goals. How can you correct this issue?
- Which aspects of your supervisory responsibilities would you like to develop this year and how can I help?
- There's a perception among some of your staff that you're more about delegating than doing. You need to turn that perception around this year. What ideas do you have for accomplishing that?
- As you take on more responsibility for employees working for you, I'd like you to develop your supervisory skills to meet the challenges that will come with that responsibility. I've enrolled you in a supervisory skills program that will meet once a week for the next three months.

Teamwork

Outstanding
- Shows exceptional teamwork
- Drives others to exceed their goals
- Works within and between teams knowledgeably and capably
- Manages the team process with great skill
- Serves as the head of _____ teams

Exceeds Expectations
- Gets along well with fellow team members
- Works well on all the teams she's a member of
- Performs team-assigned work on time and effectively
- Keeps others informed of status of projects affecting them, when responsible for doing so
- Creates strong teams

Meets Expectations
- Serves as an effective team member
- Communicates well with other teams
- Typically an optimistic team player
- Dedicated to team goals
- Heads _____ teams and serves on _____ teams

Needs Improvement
- Motivated more by his own goals than those of his team
- Not seen as a team player
- Has worked against team goals on occasion
- Fails to coordinate the work of her teams
- Was reassigned from the Safety team earlier this year

Unacceptable
- Does not work well as a teammate
- Has consistently failed to achieve goals as a team member
- Doesn't contribute much to team mission

- Does not communicate project status to affected groups when responsible for doing so
- Has been taken off _____ teams
- Other team members feel uncomfortable with her as a teammate

Self-Monitoring/Self-Evaluation

- How do you rate yourself as a team player? Tell me about the times that you were a strong member of a team. How about as a weaker contributor?
- Of all the teams you participated on this year, which do you think accomplished the most? Why?
- Some of the teams you were on had issues with teams from other divisions. How did those come about and what did you yourself do to work through these issues?
- You've been reluctant to participate on teams outside of your regular responsibilities. Why is that?

Looking Forward

- Teamwork requires support of the work of all members. Can you think of ways you can better support the work of your teammates?
- Sometimes your team has trouble coming to consensus on decisions. What decision processes could you help implement to bring about consensus?
- Are there any electronic tools your team might use to work better together? Working with your team members, would you be willing to urge their adoption?

Technical Skills

Outstanding
- Understands all work procedures and methods
- Shows technical excellence in all areas of her position
- Adapts well to technological developments relevant to her field
- Shows outstanding technical skills
- Has learned new tools to teach to others
- Uses his own time to update skills
- Maintains all certifications
- Anticipates and acquires skills before they are needed
- Creates or fixes job tools as necessary

Exceeds Expectations
- Able to learn new job-relevant skills when needed
- Demonstrates both skill and understanding of job tools
- Seen as an expert helper by peers
- Takes leadership role in acquiring new technology

Meets Expectations
- Mastered skills needed for job
- Operates job machinery effectively
- Has trouble dealing with computerized machinery
- Able to acquire and use new skills as the job requires
- Consistently follows safety and security procedures

Needs Improvement
- Retraining needed in one or two skills
- Does not have skills in problem prevention
- New technology has outstripped his existing understanding
- Lack of use has eroded a few skills

Unacceptable
- Understands very few work procedures or methods
- Demonstrates few technical skills

- Needs improvement in level of knowledge in many areas
- Has allowed certifications to lapse
- Does not alter methods to keep current with technological changes
- Lacks a majority of skills needed
- Hasn't benefited from technical skill training
- Unaware of her lack of crucial skills

Self-Monitoring/Self-Evaluation

- How are you doing keeping up with all the changes in procedures we've had this year? Are there any you've had trouble with? Why?
- Your work involves knowing so many technical details. How do you keep track of them all?
- What are you doing to make sure your staff keeps up with the rapidly changing best practices in your field?

Looking Forward

- Which of your technical skills are falling the furthest behind? How do you plan to get up to speed with them?
- There are a number of technological changes that have affected your work this year. You seem to have been caught off guard by them. How can I help you stay current with these changes so you're appropriately prepared to use them?
- Of all the seminars coming up this year, which do you think are the most important for you to attend? Will you get me a list and schedule so we can budget accordingly?
- You've done very well keeping up with all the technical aspects of your job. I'd like you to tell me where you want to focus your efforts this coming year.

Time Management Skills

Outstanding
- Rarely any wasted effort or time
- Paces herself
- Conscientiously and effectively uses time management tools
- Excellent at prioritizing tasks
- Able to deal with emergencies

Exceeds Expectations
- Never procrastinates
- Creates atmosphere for good concentration
- Works effectively with tight deadlines
- Delegates when appropriate

Meets Expectations
- Prioritizes effectively
- Usually meets deadlines
- Does not promise what can't be delivered in a specific time frame
- Manages interruptions well
- Effectively uses time management tools (e.g., planners, computers)
- Does not overextend self
- Accurately estimates how long work takes
- Outlines tasks with time line to finish overall assignment
- Breaks down task or project into workable parts

Needs Improvement
- Occasionally procrastinates
- Submitted two late reports last year
- Allows people and events to interrupt when not necessary
- Needs to use a daily planner
- Tries to do everything herself
- Is easily distracted from the task on hand
- Does not deal well with time crises

Unacceptable

- Often does not meet deadlines
- Missed four critical deadlines last year
- Easily distracted
- Does not understand how to use time management tools
- Does not prioritize tasks
- Unable to distinguish important from trivial activities
- Spends too much time socializing

Self-Monitoring/Self-Evaluation

- Do you think you're a good time manager for both yourself and your staff? Can you give me two examples?
- Which projects of yours this last year did you have the greatest challenge with managing time? Why was time management so difficult with these?
- Which time management tools do you use the most? Which do you use the least?
- You got very far behind on our project with X last year. How did that happen? What did you do? In the end, how did the project turn out?

Looking Forward

- Which time management practices do you think you need to adhere to more this year to meet the demands we're expecting?
- What can I do to help you and your staff manage time better this year?
- I'd like to see you become more proactive in your use of time rather than constantly reacting to things. How could you do this?
- I'd like to see you dedicate your time based more on the importance of a customer than on how loud they're yelling at you to get something done. What do you need to do to achieve this?

Appendix A

Ten Mistakes Managers Make When Conducting Performance Appraisals

Robert Bacal

Performance appraisals aren't fun. A lot of the time they are agonizing because many managers have some misconceptions about the process and why they do it, and the mistakes they make in light of this end up destroying a process that is important to everyone (or should be).

1. Spending more time on performance appraisal than performance *planning* or ongoing performance communication. Performance appraisal is the end of a process that goes on all the time—a process that is based on good communication between manager and employee. So, more time should be spent preventing performance problems than evaluating at the end of the year. When managers do good things during the year, the appraisal is easy to do and comfortable, because there won't be any surprises.

2. Comparing employees with each other. Want to create bad feelings, damage morale, get staff to compete so badly they will not work as a team? Then rank staff or compare staff. A guaranteed technique. And heck, not only can a manager create friction among staff, but the manager can become a great target for that hostility too. A bonus!

3. Forgetting appraisal is about improvement, not blame. We do appraisal to improve performance, not find a donkey to pin a tail on or blame. Managers who forget this end up developing staff who don't trust them, or even can't stand them. That's because the blaming process is pointless and doesn't help anyone. If there is to be a point to performance appraisal, it should be getting manager and employee working together to have everyone get better.

4. Thinking a rating form is an objective, impartial tool. Many companies use rating forms to evaluate employees (you know, the 1–5 ratings?). They do that because it's faster than doing it right. The problem comes when managers believe that those ratings are in some way "real," or anything but subjective, often vague judgments that are bound to be inaccurate. By the way, if you have two people rate the same employee, the chances of them agreeing are very small. *That's* subjective. Say it to yourself over and over. Ratings are subjective. Rating forms are subjective. Rating forms are not behavioral.

5. Stopping performance appraisal when a person's salary is no longer tied to the appraisals. Lots of managers do this. They conduct appraisals so long as they have to do so to justify or withhold a pay increase. When staff hit their salary ceiling, or pay is not connected to appraisal and performance, managers don't bother. Dumb. Performance appraisal is *for* improving performance. It isn't just about pay (although some think it is *only* about pay). If nothing else, everyone needs feedback on his or her job, whether there is money involved or not.

6. Believing they are in a position to accurately assess staff. Managers delude themselves into believing they can assess staff performance, even if they hardly ever see their staff actually doing their jobs, or the results of their jobs. Not possible. Most managers aren't in a position to monitor staff consistently enough to be able to assess well. And besides, what manager wants to do that or has the time? And, what employee wants the manager perched, watching every move? That's why appraisal is a partnership between employee and manager.

7. Cancelling or postponing appraisal meetings. Happens a whole lot. I guess because nobody likes to do them, so managers will postpone them at the drop of a hat. Why is this bad? It says to employees that the process is unimportant or phony. If managers aren't willing to commit to the process, then they shouldn't do it at all. Employees are too smart not to notice the low priority placed on appraisals.

8. Measuring or appraising the trivial. Fact of life: The easiest things to measure or evaluate are the least important things with respect to doing a job. Managers are quick to define customer service as "answering the phone within three rings" or some such thing. That's easy to measure if you want to. What's *not* easy to measure is the overall quality of service that will get and keep customers. Measuring overall customer service is hard, so many managers don't do it. But they will measure the trivial.

9. Surprising employees during appraisal. Want to really waste your time and create bad performance? This is a guaranteed technique. Don't talk to staff during the year. When they mess up, don't deal with it at the time but *save* it up. Then, at the appraisal meeting, truck out everything saved up in the bank and dump it in the employee's lap. That'll show 'em who's boss!

10. Thinking all employees and all jobs should be assessed in exactly the same way using the same procedures. Do all employees need the same things to improve their performance? Of course not. Some need specific feedback. Some don't. Some need more communication than others. And of course jobs are all different Do you think we can evaluate the CEO of Ford using the same approach we use for the person who cleans the factory floor? Of course not. So, why do managers insist on evaluating the receptionist using the same tools and criteria as the civil engineers in the office? It's not smart. One size does not fit all. Actually why do managers do this? Mostly because the personnel or human resources office leans on them to do so. It's almost understandable, but that doesn't make it any less excusable.

Appendix B

Seven Mistakes Employees Make During Performance Appraisals

Robert Bacal

Generally, when performance appraisal goes awry, the primary cause has little to do with employees. For the most part, employees take their cues from management and human resources. However, when individual employees perceive the process in negative ways, they can damage even the best of appraisal processes.

1. Focusing on the appraisal forms. Performance appraisal isn't about the forms (although, often managers and HR treat it as such). The ultimate purpose of performance appraisals is to allow employees and managers to improve continuously and to remove barriers to job success. In other words, to make everyone better. Forms don't make people better and are simply a way of recording basic information for later reference. If the focus is getting the forms "done," without thought and effort, the whole process becomes at best a waste of time, and at worst, insulting.

2. Not preparing beforehand. Preparing for performance appraisal helps the employee focus on the key issue—performance improvement—and examine his or her performance in a more objective way (see "Defensiveness" below). Unfortunately, many employees walk into the appraisal meeting not having thought about the review period, and so are unprepared to present their point of view. Being unprepared means being a reactive participant, or being a passive participant. Neither are going to help manager or employee. Employees can prepare by reviewing their work beforehand, identifying any barriers they faced in doing their job, and refamiliarizing themselves with their job description, job responsibilities, and any job performance expectations set with the manager.

3. Defensiveness. We tend to take our jobs seriously and personally, making it more difficult to hear others' comments about our work, particularly when they are critical. Even constructive criticism is often hard to hear. If employees enter into the discussion with an attitude of "defending," then it's almost impossible to create the dialogue necessary for performance improvement. That doesn't mean employees can't present their own opinions and perceptions, but it does mean that they should be presented in a calm, factual manner, rather than a defensive, emotional way. Of course, if managers are inept in the appraisal process, it makes it very difficult to avoid this defensiveness.

4. Not communicating during the year. Employees need to know how they are doing all year round, not just at appraisal time. Generally it is primarily management's responsibility to ensure that there are no surprises at appraisal time. Often managers discuss both positives and negatives of employee performance throughout the year, but this is unfortunately not a universal practice. It's in the employees' interests to open up discussion about performance during the year, even if the manager does not initiate it. The sooner employees know where they are and what they need to change (or keep doing), the sooner problems can be fixed. In fact many problems can be prevented if they are caught early enough. Even if managers aren't creating that communication, employees can and should. It's a shared responsibility.

5. Not clarifying enough. Life would be much easier if managers were perfect, but they aren't. Some communicate and explain well. Some don't. Some are aggravating and some not. At times employees won't be clear about their manager's reasoning or comments, or what a manager is suggesting. That could be because the manager isn't clear himself/herself, or simply isn't good at explaining. However, unless employees clarify when they aren't sure about the reasoning or explanations, they won't know what they need to do to improve their future job performance. It's important to leave the appraisal meeting having a good understanding of what's been said. If that's not possible, clarification can occur after the meeting, or down the road, if that's more appropriate.

6. Allowing one-sidedness. Performance appraisals work best when both participants are active and expressing their positions and ideas. Some employees are uncomfortable doing that, and while managers should be creating a climate where employees are comfortable, some managers aren't good at it. Performance appraisal time is an excellent time for employees to make suggestions about things that could be changed to improve performance, about how to remove barriers to job success, and about ways to increase productivity. Remember also that managers can't read minds. The better managers will work with employees to help them do their jobs more effectively, but they can't know how they can help unless employees provide them with good, factual information or, even better, concrete ideas.

7. Focusing on the appraisal as a way of getting more money.
Unfortunately, many organizations tie employee pay to appraisal results, which puts employee and manager on opposite sides. Employees in such systems tend to focus too much on the money component, although that focus is certainly understandable. It's also understandable when employees in such systems become hesitant to reveal shortcomings or mistakes. But it's still dumb. If employees' main purpose is to squeeze as much of an increase out of the company, and the managers try to keep increases as small as possible, it becomes totally impossible to focus on what ultimately matters over the long term, which is continuous performance improvement and success for everyone.

Pay *is* important, but it is not the only issue related to the appraisal focus. If employees enter into the process willing to defend their own positions in factual and fair ways and to work with managers, the process can become much more pleasant. If not, it can become a war.

Conclusion

The major responsibilities for setting performance appraisal tone and climate rest with managers and the human resources department. However, even when managers and human resources do their jobs well, employees who come at the process with a negative or defensive approach are not likely to gain from the process or to prosper over the long term. The constant key is for employees to participate actively and assertively, but to keep a problem-solving mind-set and keep focused on how things can be improved in the future. No matter who initiates it, performance appraisal is about positive open communication between employee and manager.

About the Authors

Douglas Max is managing director, LR Communication Systems, Inc., in Berkeley Heights, New Jersey. He is responsible for all marketing and sales, selection, training, and supervision of a staff of 15. His firm designs and conducts on-site and online programs in business writing and presentation skills. He formerly "owned" and moderated TRDEV, the largest training-oriented e-mail discussion group on the Web. He has a B.A. from Washington University in St. Louis and an M.A. in Industrial/Organizational Psychology from the University of Missouri at St. Louis. Doug lives in Berkeley Heights, New Jersey, with his wife, Nora, and two sons, Xander (a great golfer) and Emerson (a great skateboarder).

Robert Bacal is an accomplished consultant, book author, trainer, and public speaker. He is the author of *Perfect Phrases for Setting Performance Goals*, *Perfect Phrases for Managing Your Small Business* (with Nancy Moore), *Manager's Guide to Performance Reviews*, *Managing Performance*, and several other books. He is an active management consultant and popular speaker. His website, **www.work911.com**, includes many articles and other materials to help managers across many fields and tasks.

The Right Phrase for Every Situation...Every Time

Perfect Phrases for Building Strong Teams
Perfect Phrases for Business Letters
Perfect Phrases for Business Proposals and Business Plans
Perfect Phrases for Business School Acceptance
Perfect Phrases for College Application Essays
Perfect Phrases for Cover Letters
Perfect Phrases for Customer Service
Perfect Phrases for Dealing with Difficult People
Perfect Phrases for Dealing with Difficult Situations at Work
Perfect Phrases for Documenting Employee Performance Problems
Perfect Phrases for Executive Presentations
Perfect Phrases for Landlords and Property Managers
Perfect Phrases for Law School Acceptance
Perfect Phrases for Lead Generation
Perfect Phrases for Managers and Supervisors
Perfect Phrases for Managing Your Small Business
Perfect Phrases for Medical School Acceptance
Perfect Phrases for Meetings
Perfect Phrases for Motivating and Rewarding Employees
Perfect Phrases for Negotiating Salary & Job Offers
Perfect Phrases for Perfect Hiring
Perfect Phrases for the Perfect Interview
Perfect Phrases for Performance Reviews
Perfect Phrases for Real Estate Agents & Brokers
Perfect Phrases for Resumes
Perfect Phrases for Sales and Marketing Copy
Perfect Phrases for the Sales Call
Perfect Phrases for Sales Presentations
Perfect Phrases for Setting Performance Goals
Perfect Phrases for Small Business Owners
Perfect Phrases for the TOEFL Speaking and Writing Sections
Perfect Phrases for Writing Company Announcements
Perfect Phrases for Writing Grant Proposals
Perfect Phrases in American Sign Language for Beginners
Perfect Phrases in French for Confident Travel
Perfect Phrases in German for Confident Travel
Perfect Phrases in Italian for Confident Travel
Perfect Phrases in Spanish for Confident Travel to Mexico
Perfect Phrases in Spanish for Construction
Perfect Phrases in Spanish for Gardening and Landscaping

Visit mhprofessional.com/perfectphrases for a complete product listing.

Learn more. McGraw Hill Do more.

THE IDEAL PERFORMANCE SUPPORT SOLUTION FOR MANAGERS AND SUPERVISORS

With over 30,000 phrases, *Perfect Phrases for Managers* is an unmatched digital resource that provides managers at every level with the skills they need to effectively manage any situation.

From performance reviews to documenting problems, to motivating and coaching teams, to managing difficult people and embarrassing situations, this performance support tool will help your company create an environment for exceptional performance.

Go to **www.perfectphrases.com** to learn more about *Perfect Phrases for Managers* and how you can access:

- A "Things to Consider" section with hundreds of bite-size coaching tips
- Audio clips from actual conversations
- Strategies for opening up healthy communication

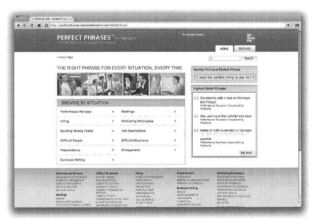

The right phrase for every situation, every time.

Visit www.perfectphrases.com to learn how your company can qualify for a trial subscription.

11118515R00129

Made in the USA
San Bernardino, CA
08 May 2014